. . . 1914

Books by James Cameron:

Mandarin Red
1914

JAMES CAMERON

Rinehart & Company, Inc., New York

Grateful acknowledgment is made to The Public Trustee and The Society of Authors, London, England, for permission to reprint an excerpt from a letter of Bernard Shaw's which first appeared in the London *Daily News*.

FOREWORD

Sometimes the half-remembered has more compelling associations than either the familiar or the unknown; there is a period of time suspended between the remote and the only-yesterday that has a special meaning in a contemporary breakneck world that seems to offer no choice of contemplation between an inaccessible past and a highly dubious future.

The intention of this book is to tell the simple story of a year in the life of Britain—and, to some degree, of Europe—that more than any other year in the memory of men now living can be considered the close of an era. In the year 1914 the world, as it was known and accepted then, came to an end. Far more than any year before or since was this the punctuation-mark of the twentieth century. It was the end of many things that were bad and perhaps even more that were good; both the good and the bad contributed to the climax. Out of the crucible of the First World War came something that could variously be defined as either an improvement or a corruption of the smooth days before; at least they were wholly and irretrievably changed. The year

1914 was itself only partially responsible, partially symbolic of the watershed. Nevertheless it was on that late summer day in 1914 that Sir Edward Grey, and many men less sensitive and obsessed, knew that from then on nothing could ever be the same.

This is a direct narrative, without any especial analysis or philosophy; particularly have I tried to avoid too much hindsight, or giving to events as they occurred then the extra emphasis, or glamour, or piquancy that so many of them acquired later in the light of the bleak paradoxes that were to come.

The number of things this book does not affect to be could fill a chapter. Chiefly, however, it is not a war book, though war must necessarily inform it throughout. It is not a work of scholarship, of which there are, fortunately for me, already scores. Its politics and economics and military records are in the main only those that affected everybody. It can hardly be a personal reminiscence—at this strange time I was three years old, and the handfuls of elusive images I sometimes seem to recall must surely be induced by the authentic memories of others. (I do not claim that I really took the salute from a regimental contingent of Canadian troops marching through a Buckinghamshire village on their way to the front, yet that is one of my unshakable fantasies, as vivid and as improbable as that of meeting my father's heroine, the late Marie Lloyd.)

I have of course done this book out of other books. To name all the many records that have made it possible is out of the question—a note here, a phrase there, an anecdote emerging from irrelevancies, a long immersion in the newspaper files of the time—but a list of the major and essential sources is appended. I deeply acknowledge my debt to them and to all the others on the back of whose greater researches this book is built.

"1914" is presented, as the painters then reaching the zenith of their popularity would have done, as an impressionist picture of the latter half of a momentous year in the life of a people who, for good or ill, were never to see their world again as they saw it then.

J. C.

. . . 1914

That year the summer came ungrudgingly early, glowing and serene, taking its temper from the strangely sanguine and tranquil mood of the country, a sense of common optimism itself still new enough to be savoured and valued.

It was a summer of especial splendour. For once even the English sky accorded with the cloudless humour of the nation and enhanced it, day followed day in golden composure; all over the kingdom things were going well. Never before had Europe presented a face so prosperous and buoyant. In England particularly it was possible to look at the future with confidence. It even seemed that at last the whole community could share in some degree this felicity—Social Reform had arrived to ease cares here, and consciences there. A programme of Old Age Pensions and Insurance Schemes had officially freed the poor from some, at least, of the ghosts that had haunted them (or should have done, since it was costing £22,000,000 a year). The plague of strikes and lockouts that had convulsed the country two years before was over. All this greatly encouraged the rich to believe in the theory of absolute progress; it was an enlightened age and the Liberal Party was its prophet. One might not like the Liberals, but there they were, apparently immovable (so long as the Irishmen behaved), pointing blandly to achievements all around.

Not only was the future full of promise; the present itself was a thing for congratulation, and if a moment's uncertainty should intervene, the record was there for all to examine—look at the motor car, look at the Marconi telegraph, look at the flying-machine, look at Mr Shaw, look at Sir Thomas Lipton, look at the Labour Exchanges. To be sure, most of this had to be paid for, and income tax had reached the unprecedented rate of 1s 4d in the pound. The ebullient and slightly questionable Lloyd George was the symbol both of adventure and of a certain doubt —however, it could not be denied that the financial year had ended triumphantly for the Welshman, and vindicated that aggressive optimism. Without increasing taxation he had budgeted for £194,825,000 and produced a surplus of £185,000. If the poor were not thankful for their advantages they should have been; they had only to look back to the barbarities of the previous century, before a humane administration occupied itself with their redemption and rationalised their unavoidable misfortunes. But politics, bitter and furious enough in Westminster, existed outside it only for the smoking-rooms or at the drawing-room level, and then only where dedicated hostesses like Lady Londonderry or Mrs Asquith permitted themselves to make a social issue of the Home Rule Bill, or dispute the memory of the People's Budget.

War was scarcely even a speculation, nor had been since all was fulfilled and settled in South Africa a decade ago—and that, for all the passions engendered, had been far away and, on the whole, not wholly ungallant in its resolution. There had, indeed, been a brief point of danger, a momentary catching of the breath at Agadir, but that, too, was three years past.

Western Europe had known no war for close on two generations, and though the Balkans muttered and grumbled in their endless incomprehensible dynastic feuds these considerations were obscure and meaningless to any but those whose business it was to study them, remotely and abstractly, as one might observe the fretful behaviour of bees. The Turkish revolution had exposed all manner of weaknesses and inflammations, involving interests as complex as their names:—Austria-Hungary had seized Bosnia-Herzegovina; Italy had seized Tripoli; the Balkan States had forced a humiliation on the Ottomans and had forthwith fallen to fighting among themselves, with Serbia and Greece gnawing at the carcass of Turkey. Sir Edward Grey would put all that nonsense right, everyone said. Grey could bear down on the presumptions and contentions of places like Montenegro and Albania; he was the man to keep Austria and Russia in line, and that was the only thing that mattered. In no conceivable way could these mountebank activities touch the secure pattern of London life in those auspicious days.

The 1914 Season, like that of the year before, had been of a singular brilliance. Not for many years, if ever, had the social scene shone with such a lustre, such a montage of tiaras and white gloves, such a stimulating restless abundance of champagne and rare flowers, such rewarding expenditure on things of the flesh and, indeed, of the mind also. London felt itself suddenly a capital, its well-to-do inhabitants aware equally of the affairs of Paris, Vienna, St. Petersburg, absorbing new trends in the arts as readily as those in fashion, for culture was both nourishing and modish, and half the social world, as Walter Sickert said, "dined out for Art."

The opera and the ballet blossomed, mostly under the urge of that thirty-five-year-old zealot Mr Thomas Beecham. They reached an apotheosis under the influences of the new lions: Stravinsky, Karsavina, Fokine, Diaghilev, Nijinsky. A public already startled by the savage strident impact of *Le Sacre du Printemps* had that summer been given, through the lucky presence together in London of two great Russian companies of opera and ballet, the unprecedented spectacle of *Le Coq d'Or*. Melba had opened the opera season in the Garden with *La Bohème*, and Albert Coates became the first Englishman ever to conduct it. There was the first night of Zandonai's *Francesca da Rimini*. The Music Club announced a party for the fiftieth birthday of Richard Strauss, in the presence of Igor Stravinsky, Feodor Chaliapin, Claude Debussy, Frederick Delius. . . .

Foreigners abounded, of an acceptable kind, which most were, being rich. It was hard to entertain the old resentment of aliens when so clearly they entertained no such thing themselves. London was full of cultivated Germans—their Ambassador Lichnowsky was uncommonly cordial, and much sought after, and his Kaiser would scarcely have paid so many visits to his cousin in Buckingham Palace if he had designs against England's well-being. He had, it was true, been crude and discourteous in the past; he had written an indiscreet letter of encouragement to Britain's enemy Kruger in 1895, but he grew daily more civilised. The Russians, too, would one day develop and mature under the example of the Czar into a liberal and well-managed people. If foreigners came to England, obviously they came to admire. . . . It was true that not all were rich; among the others who had passed through not long ago was a small and lightly-bearded Slav with Jewish eyes in a Tartar face, who saw in this elegant scene something for which he alone could write the final alternative, and whose name was Vladimir Ilyich Ulianov, or, as he chose to be called, Lenin. He intruded in no way on this comfortable world, nor was to do so until it had already gone.

Fashion meant the new names from Paris—Paquin and Worth, Doucet, Drécol, the Boué Soeurs, and with Paul Poiret actually presenting a collection in Number 10 Downing Street, by courtesy of Mrs Asquith. A hat was not a hat but, perhaps, a Watteau, a spreading confection in straw in the smart new shade of *ficelle*, or string, trimmed with crêpe and tea-roses. Aigrettes were greatly in demand. There arrived the hobble skirt. . . . That year a Mr James H. Wilson, in the Bond Street lingerie business as "Maud Taylor," was examined in bankruptcy; he claimed that his failure was due to the fact that women no longer wore underclothes.

The theatre was vividly alive. Though Henry Irving was nine years dead and Bernhardt an old woman, their personalities still informed the reviews of William Archer. Mr Bernard Shaw's *Pygmalion* had just opened at His Majesty's, with Mrs Campbell as Eliza and Sir Herbert Tree as Higgins, and the adventurous word *bloody* sent a *frisson* of startled pleasure all over town, among an intelligentsia already warming to eccentricity in the arts.

The exhibition of French Post-Impressionists, and the Futurists, had opened many an eye adjusted to Orpen, Sickert, Steer—but already Wyndham Lewis was editing *Blast* on behalf of the Vorticists and declaring that Post-Impressionism was in limbo, and Futurism a thing of the past.

The march of the moderns had begun even to penetrate the smarter drawing-rooms. In Streatham and Hammersmith a home would be decently equipped only with overmantels, brass hearth furniture, fretwork pipe-racks, pianolas with fronts of pleated silk, chenille tablecloths, prints by Landseer and Japanese jars, but in South Kensington and Curzon Street it was proper for everything to reflect the fantasies of Benois and Bakst, or the orange-skirted gipsy women of the young Augustus John.

One read immensely—the books tumbled from the presses at six shillings a time, and that summer more prodigiously than ever. It was the age of high and abundant romance—Charles Garvice's *The Woman's Way*, W. J.

Locke's *Fortunate Youth*, Baroness Orczy's *Unto Caesar*. Miss Ethel M. Dell gave birth to *The Swindler*, Miss Marie Corelli to *The Innocent*. John Galsworthy continued his relentless examination of the middle-class scene, finding, as though ruefully, seeds of social injustice even in the country houses. Arnold Bennett revealed his world of Midland mercers and Grand Hotels—his *Price of Love* had just begun a serial version in the *Daily News*, in instalments of diminishing size, as by and by vaster issues were to encroach on the page, until one day it vanished altogether, replaced by a Kitchener recruiting appeal. Still, there was a new Sherlock Holmes in the *Strand Magazine*. A curious Irish newcomer called James Joyce published *Dubliners*— not without long and exasperating difficulties; ten years earlier the printers had refused to set it, alleging uncountable libels. At last Grant Richards had managed to publish it, at 3s 6d, without much applause. "To recognise quality in Mr Joyce," said a reviewer, "is not to have discovered a genius. Mr Joyce, young in years, is old and embittered in spirit. . . ." Two months later he was busy, surrounded with old Dublin newspapers, tram-tickets, handbills and letters from which he was building a complex mosaic called *Ulysses;* the business was interrupted by simpler international difficulties of which he was barely aware.

There was H. G. Wells, with his scientific heroes and emancipated mistresses with becoming useful tweeds and serious hazel eyes. This year he published an imaginative work called *The World Set Free*, in which he described a fantastic and fortunately improbable bomb which (the things the man thought of!) released the power of the atom. . . .

Another power, more tangible if no less fanciful, was striving for release: some women had discovered, or dreamed, a new destiny for themselves, simultaneously dedicated and somehow ridiculous, an eccentricity, a passion and indeed a martyrdom. The Suffragettes had been at work for nearly four years, since 1910; by now they were to be taken deadly seriously. Long before, Mrs Emmeline Pankhurst, widow of a Lancashire barrister, had founded the Women's Social and Political Union, and one Private Member's Bill for the legitimising of votes for women had actually reached the floor of the House, and had been submerged in a stream of masculine irony.

In the summer of 1914 Mrs Pankhurst's adherents were a formidable army. They were to be recognised by the new Reasonable clothes, their hard starched collars and their shirt-waists, their straw boaters—some said they cultivated an undigested masculinity, and claimed to detect vaguely lesbian trends. They had, to be sure, abandoned the negative legacy of "female security," the emptiness of the Perfect Wife—conceiving children without desire, rearing them without delight. If she were unmarried, there was nothing. Mrs Pankhurst, who had pondered this for years, finally exploded—there was no point in a franchise legislation that grew from some sort of political charity: "a woman's hand about the House." The Suffragettes went into business the hard way.

London by now had become uneasily familiar with

the strange processions—the long straight skirts, the feathered hats, the faces abashed or defiant—the Downing Street pickets, the sudden eruptions from the gallery of the House. The Suffragettes chained themselves to railings, they burned "Votes For Women" with acid into the well-bred turf of golf-course greens, they attacked Bellini's "Agony in the Garden" in the National Gallery. They submitted to the rough and sometimes savage handling of the police, the mockery of the rowdies. There were Mrs Pethwick Lawrence, Miss Christabel Pankhurst and her sister Sylvia—there was Emily Wilding Davidson, arrested in Parliament Street as she tried to push a torch of burning paraffin into the Post Office letter-box, who then went on hunger-strike, was forcibly fed, deluged with water by hosepipe in her cell—and who was at last to die under the hooves of the King's horse at Epsom in the Derby of June 1913. . . . Soon people ceased to laugh.

Other women danced—for dancing was the new thing, in its many varieties of form: on the one hand Isadora Duncan had emerged in Europe from San Francisco, mystically clothed in white draperies, providing the dance with a splendid sensuality under a cover of classicism; on the other hand the thudding music of the Negroes who had taken over the dance-bands, and the girls in their Scheherazade skirts practised the intricacies of the tango, the bunny hug, the turkey trot, the maxixe. . . .

And in any case there were Little Tich at the Palladium, Elsie Janis and Nelson Keyes at the Palace, Violet Lorraine at the Hippodrome. There were *Potash and*

Perlmutter and *Kismet* and *When Knights Were Bold* and *The Belle of New York*. There were Owen Nares and Oscar Asche and H. B. Irving and Maskelyne and Devant. In the Kingsway there was now one of the new Bioscopes: *Harry Lauder Among The Mormons*. The Great White City, last descendant of the pleasure-gardens of Cremorne, Vauxhall, Ranelagh, proclaimed the Anglo-American Exposition: "Wonders of the Panama Canal—The Grand Canyon—America's Sky Scrapers."

Everyone said it was bound to be a fine Bank Holiday.

. . . 2

The Liberal Party of England had been in office for most of nine years. It had first come to power with the biggest mandate since the Parliament of the Cavaliers, and now it depended for its existence on the goodwill, impulse, caprice or stratagem of eighty Irishmen in the House of Commons.

At the head stood Herbert Henry Asquith, the Yorkshire lawyer, the able, reflective, cautious and monumentally reliable man who was secure on all things and passionate on none: the Moderate. He was defined at the time as "moderately Imperialist, moderately humorous, moderately progressive, and, being the most fastidious of Liberal politicians, only moderately evasive." The Party was swinging to the right, but only in moderation. It looked ahead, but not intemperately. Mr Asquith in Downing Street was in harness with the exuberant demagogue Lloyd George, but nothing indecorously radical infiltrated through the wall to Number Ten.

Then there was the King. For four years George V had been on the throne, modestly and obstinately, well aware that as far as a popular monarchy went he had started from behind the line. He had taken over with few advantages; he had succeeded a personality of broad appeal. What his father had ever actually accomplished was never clear to anyone; nevertheless he had been enwrapped in a tolerant mythology. He had displayed all the admirable qualities of the bourgeois hedonist—he was jovial, sensual, indulgent, just disreputable enough to be reassuring. In time to come it was to be easy enough to take Edward VII to pieces in popular Freudian terms, as a male heir frustrated by a dominant mother, herself compensating for a legally impotent Consort and husband by exercising a traditionally male authority, revealing a curious jealousy of Edward as successor, crippling him by repressive education. All in all, Edward emerged rather well, by the uncomplicated standards of his time.

He was perhaps hardly the man to have been confronted by such a paradoxical world: socially so settled, so convivial, politically so divided, and with the storm-clouds already gathering outside, built by an accumulation of forty years of German diplomatic follies matched by parallel blunderings elsewhere. To Edward VII, Europe, after all, was a simple grouping of large family estates preponderantly governed by relatives. It was necessary to Edward that German policies should be impeded wherever possible, if only somehow to express his resentment of his mother's affection for all things German, to make manifest his liberation from the dreary days of tutelage as Prince of Wales, and in face of his nephew's plain contempt of him.

Young Willie had to be put in his place; therefore the King would respond readily to all international relationships that helped to that end.

George V succeeded to the throne in his forty-fifth year, after eighteen years as heir presumptive. He was still, by the ebullient standards of his father, an amateur. He had been fifteen years in the Navy and had seen the world—or, as was sometimes said, he had seen quite a few coaling stations in various places. At home he may have been "a short-tempered Tory." If so, he was unchallengeably respectable. Marlborough House had been a very austere establishment indeed; now Buckingham Palace would be even more so. The politicians, wholly uninterested in his personal virtues, were far more concerned that the King would be an easy victim to Tory blandishments.

It was several years before they were to learn that George V was a good king.

Even in those anodyne days it was often argued that so long as Europe was constituted in its familiar idiot fashion the balance of danger existed. Many felt that the moment of truth had come after the Franco-Prussian War of 1870: if Bismarck had not demanded from France the surrender of Alsace-Lorraine (over and above the £700,-000,000 indemnity), history could have taken a simpler course. France might not have been driven in her rancour and bitterness to start rebuilding her Army; Germany might not then have tried to quarantine her. But Bismarck compelled Wilhelm I in 1879 to form the Dual Alliance with Austria-Hungary, in which both states agreed on mutual support against a Russian attack, and neutrality in the event of an attack by a third party. When that treaty, till then secret, was published in 1888 it was clear that the division of Europe into two camps was complete. The inevitable Franco-Russian Alliance was just as full of peril, since any ill-considered move by Austria in the Balkans would lead to Russian mobilisation, and the automatic entry of both Germany and France, on opposing sides, in a conflict that would be impossible to contain.

"The Kaiser is a profoundly pacific man," wrote Baron Beyens, the Belgian Minister to Berlin, "but the spirit of the German governing classes is very different. They hate France and believe only in the greatness of Germany."

There appeared a sensational article in the *Kölnische Zeitung* from its correspondent in St. Petersburg: "By 1917 the Russian Army reforms will be complete and her troops massed on the western border. Russian armaments are enormous. Germany will perhaps not be able to avoid invasion."

When later that summer of 1914, President Wilson of the United States sent his personal emissary, Colonel House, to Berlin to investigate the chances of an Anglo-German-American entente, House was startled by the atmosphere of growing militarism he found there. "The whole of Germany is charged with electricity," he wrote, "it only needs a spark to set the whole thing off." He came to

London, and was alarmed and exasperated by what he felt was ignorance and indifference.

Then Germany raised a capital levy of £50,000,000, and German firms began calling in moneys due from abroad, wherever possible in gold. France raised her military service from two years to three. The Russian Duma increased her recruiting from 450,000 to 580,000 men a year, to a strength of 2,500,000 men. There was, if one had known it, no going back.

In April the King paid a state visit to Paris, the first of his protocol complimentary trips. For this reason or that it had been troublesome before; this time it was propitious enough—the Entente endured, though it was well known that France was deeply concerned by what seemed an alarming intimacy between Sir Edward Grey and the German Ambassador in London, Lichnowsky. It was largely to settle these doubts that the King took Sir Edward Grey with him to Paris.

It was the first time during all his long office that the British Secretary of State for Foreign Affairs had ever left his native land.

The weather smiled; the chestnut flowers glowed; in the state procession the King rode beside President Poincaré in the first coach, Grey with Prime Minister-Foreign Secretary Doumergue in the second. No one spoke a word of politics.

Then on the final day Grey was invited to the Quai

d'Orsay, and the real proposition clearly put. France, while content with British relations as they were, was less so with her attitude to France's allies, the Russians. The French and British General Staffs were in formal consultation. Why should Britain not do the same for the Russians? The navies at least should co-operate—not that the French set any great store on the Russian Navy (which in the event of a German war could not get out of the Baltic anyway), but because it would conciliate St. Petersburg.

Sir Edward Grey, puzzled, vaguely alarmed at the French insistence, and still determined on principle not to turn any old Ententes into Alliances, at last agreed to the gesture of consulting the Russians. These discussions, enthusiastic though they may have been, were still incomplete four months later, and by that time it was far too late.

For years, it seemed in 1914 to those who cared, British politics had been dominated by two things: the Irishmen and the Peers. With the death of Edward VII the clandestine struggle with the House of Lords had been driven into the open; the fresh air was already killing it. The Lords' case rested on the double proposition, traditionally unchallengeable, that the aristocracy must be (a) powerful and (b) responsible. The counter argument was even simpler: since the aristocracy was socially moribund and historically diminishing, it must be curbed. Two forces leaned tediously one against the other: the middle-class philosophy which was called liberalism, and the landed wealth which nowadays passed for aristocracy and which sought its symbolism in an Upper House whose powers had been already curtailed.

Many people detected in both the thin sad scent of dissolution.

Others foresaw even grimmer spectres. "Socialism is a nebulous flaccidity of parasitic thought!" (Thus a broadsheet from a Mr John Littlejohns, of Pontypridd.) "Mr W. Churchill is the biggest braggart of blatant braggadoccio in the brutish trituration of bombastic Radicalism! Mr Lloyd George addresses public meetings with the grimace of a Mountebank and the spite of a Viper. The present Government is a mawkish medley of parasitical lugubriousness!" cried Mr Littlejohns, warming to his work, "a neurotic contemporary amalgam of mental profligacy, which seeks to disintegrate the Empire with persuasive pasquinades, Liberal levity, volatile vivacity, and designed deception. . . ."

The Irish question, however, dominated everything; throughout that delectable spring of 1914 it grew almost daily more threatening, the spectre behind every political attitude, every domestic alignment. In the Commons the two parties were fairly enough matched, and Asquith owed his continuance only to the support of forty Labour members, who mattered not much, and to that of the eighty Irish Nationalists, who mattered greatly. If the Liberals continued to govern by courtesy of the Irish members, the price to pay was the Home Rule Bill.

John Redmond, who had succeeded Parnell as Irish Nationalist leader after the sad scandals of the O'Shea divorce over twenty years before, had agreed with Asquith on the common principle of a united Nationalist Ireland. Many impediments to this had gone, including the constitutional veto of the Lords. So long as the Lords could throw out Home Rule as often as the Commons presented it, and keep it off the Statute Book as they had done with Gladstone's Bill, the Liberals must plead for patience from the Irishmen. But the Lords' wings were clipped. Moreover Ireland was herself a better proposition today; by the Wyndham Land Act of Balfour's last Conservative Government, in 1903, the more obvious economic wrongs had been put right, or were about to be so; going was the offence of the absentee landlords and the ascendancy of the ignorant squireens. Had Ireland only been united— but of course no country was less united, but rather deeply divided in the most passionate bitterness of all.

North of Catholic Ireland stood Protestant Ulster, dour and determined, beating its knuckles on the Orange Drums, remembering the Battle of the Boyne when King Billy laid James II low—contemptuous of Catholics yet fearing a priestly despotism ("Home Rule means Rome Rule!"); thrifty, assured, determined, charmless, loyal to Ulster and to nothing else, equating everything, from the Crown to the Empire, only with their insular security.

"The crown o' the causeway on road or street," they sang, "and the population under our feet!"

Ulster would resist Home Rule—literally to the death, they cried. John Redmond, visiting the United States, had told an audience of Chicago Hibernians: "Not an Irishman in America today would not rejoice to hear that a German Army was marching in triumph across England from Yarmouth to Milford Haven!" From a hundred obscure places in Britain, from small-time barbers and ice-cream dealers and Diplomatic Secretaries the messages went back to the European Foreign Offices: the United Kingdom, if you could call it such, is riddled with dissension; indeed there is the considerable likelihood of civil war.

This was studied with interest in the Wilhelmstrasse.

The English Tories found little to love in all this, but it was clearly a good whip with which to flog the Liberals. Liberals! cried the Tories—Chapel Liberals, preparing to drive the Protestant Irish into the Papist arms! Andrew Bonar Law, too, began to beat the Orange Drum. He was a humourless Scots-Canadian Presbyterian, whose father stemmed from an Ulster manse. When Balfour had grown "too tired," as he said, Bonar Law had taken over the Tory—or Unionist—leadership. Asquith had described him as "meekly ambitious."

When it was clear that Asquith was formally allied to the Irish Nationalists—Redmond and Dillon and Wee Joe Devlin—Ulster went Unionist to a man, and behind the banner was Sir Edward Carson.

Carson KC was a Southern Irishman, as it happened, MP for Dublin University; nevertheless he was a fanatic Protestant. In 1914, at the age of sixty, he was making a handsome fortune at the English bar—his ruthless, skilful prosecution of Oscar Wilde had already brought him fame.

He suffered from ambition, nerves, insomnia, poor digestion, insatiable energy. He recruited the "Ulster Volunteers." From the Protestant landowners, farmers, squires, ex-militia officers he built up an army of 100,000, drilled them with rifles; by and by they were to have machine-guns, ambulances, transport, organisation. Carson said: "The cost may be great; the sufferings may be terrible."

In Balmoral, a suburb of Belfast, the Volunteers broke out and saluted a Union Jack forty-eight feet by twenty-five—the biggest flag, it was said, ever made in the world.

In the South the Home Rulers naturally formed their own "National Army." It was just as illegal as the Volunteers, but less well equipped. Civil war was round the corner. Already a Civil War Indemnity Fund of a million pounds had been raised for the Volunteers.

Partition seemed the only answer. It was hardly possible without a transfer of populations, but it could have been done, accepting the Liberal principle of self-determination. Yet for the Liberals to concede that meant the sacrifice of the Irish Nationalist support in the Commons, and that was too needful.

An enormous demonstration was mounted in Hyde Park; fourteen platforms were erected between the Serpentine and Bayswater Road, to which converged twenty-two processions "to protest against the use of the Army and Navy against fellow-subjects in Ireland." Members of the Carlton, the Junior Carlton, the Constitutional, and the Junior Constitutional Clubs marched together; the park was full of silk hats, Union Jacks and Peers. There was the

Ladies' Imperial Club, and delegations from the Stock Exchange and Lloyd's. There were speeches from Carson, Austen Chamberlain, Milner, F. E. Smith, Robert Cecil, and Arthur Balfour, making the first and last Hyde Park speech of his correct and urbane life.

In the middle of all this King George wrote from Sandringham to Lord Stamfordham:

> I confess I am greatly concerned. . . . I am perfectly prepared to take the proper responsibility which belongs to the Sovereign of this country, but I shall continue as long as I can to persuade the parties concerned to agree, and I shall certainly do all in my power to prevent Civil War and bloodshed in Ireland. . . . The more I think of it all, the more worried I get. . . .

The King took the whole situation very seriously; he saw the Prime Minister at Windsor and suggested that a General Election might clear the air. Mr Asquith said it would do nothing of the kind; on the contrary it could not possibly settle anything. The King replied that while he recognised that as a Constitutional Sovereign he was not responsible for whatever confusions his Ministers should create, nevertheless he could not allow bloodshed in any of his Dominions without exerting every means in his power to avert it. He would see the Premier at any time, or he would send for Bonar Law—or even Carson, for that matter. He would risk being rebuffed—did anyone realise the predicament the Crown would be in should there be civil war?

That same afternoon Bonar Law moved a vote of

censure on the Government. While the debate was in progress Carson very pointedly and obviously left the House, with a most grim demeanour. It was greatly feared that he had walked out just in time to catch the Night Mail to Belfast, and that at any moment he might proclaim a Provisional Government of Ireland. That was the cue for what was then and shall forever be known as the Curragh Mutiny.

On 14th March, British reinforcements were sent to protect military stores at Carrickfergus. It was thought probable that the Great Northern Railway of Ireland might well refuse to carry the troops—such was the nervous state of the administration—so it was decided to send the troops by sea, and to move the 3rd battle-squadron to Lamlash in Arran, within reach of Ireland. These were, unquestionably, dispositions for civil war. The Army was in a condition of anguished uncertainty, as well it might be, since many of its officers were either Anglo-Irish or of Ulster associations. Clearly they would resent the duty of forcing northern Protestants to submit to southern Catholics—if the Home Rule Bill became law, and if the Ulster leaders, the Carsonites, resisted by force, they could well be ordered to suppress a technical rebellion. What would that mean but the necessity of British troops to shoot down Ulstermen for the crime of being loyal to Britain? It was obvious that great numbers of officers would send in their papers rather than fight under Government orders, and the Opposition Front Bench was urging them on.

This impossible dilemma was crystallised when the

War Office instructed Sir Arthur Paget, General Officer Commanding Ireland, to assemble his officers at the Curragh and tell them that, in the event of genuine trouble, any officer domiciled in Ireland could with permission opt out for the duration of the operation; any others with conscientious scruples should express them, and forthwith be dismissed the service.

Nothing of the kind had, perhaps, ever been known in any army before. It split the service from top to bottom. Lord Roberts openly supported the Ulster volunteers; so did Sir Henry Wilson, Director of Military Operations at the War Office, himself an Anglo-Irishman. Brigadier-General Hubert Gough and fifty-seven out of seventy officers of the 3rd Cavalry Brigade announced that they would prefer dismissal to acceptance of the order to move north. Gough's brother John, who was Haig's Chief of Staff in the Aldershot Command, proclaimed that he would leave the Army. The Conservatives in the House of Lords made public their proposal to amend the Mutiny Act. The most tremendous row blew up in Parliament: the Conservatives accused the Government of planning a massacre of Ulster loyalists; the Liberals replied that the Tories were openly supporting rebellion and seducing officers from their loyal allegiance. The whole English party system was in the most acute danger—to the singular satisfaction of every German agent in the country, and they were many, who happily and accurately reported back that England was tormented by strife, in the hopeless grip of factions.

Finally the Cabinet was compelled to find its formula: in future, they wrote down, soldiers should not be asked to find answers to hypothetical questions; they must, however, obey lawful orders.

Gough, secretly advised by Sir Henry Wilson, demanded assurances that there would be no question of coercing Ulster. Colonel Seely, the Secretary of State for War, added two paragraphs to the State document giving that assurance, without consulting his colleagues. They were immediately repudiated by Asquith. Seely resigned. Sir John French, the Chief of the Imperial General Staff, and Sir Spencer Ewart, Adjutant-General—both of whom had approved and initialled the addenda—resigned too. The entire British military organisation was in disarray. The King complained to the Prime Minister that he had not been informed of these drastic developments; he sent for Sir John French and said that "if great tact is not shewn there will shortly be no Army left." Carson's Volunteers, secretly mobilised, managed to land 25,000 rifles and 1,000,-000 rounds at Larne. The Cabinet considered prosecuting Carson, and proclaiming a treasonable conspiracy; only the urgent arguments of John Redmond held their hand.

Thus was the British situation, three months from the greatest war in history.

So abrupt, so shocking was the impact of this dissension that its very urgency brought its own sedative; by the beginning of June an understanding seemed almost possible. At least negotiations were down to a detailed level—partition was inevitable, depending on a simple geographical decision: should the borderline areas of Fermanagh and Tyrone be included in Ulster or not?

All this was noted and recorded by the German Foreign Office with interest and appreciation. The Ambassador Lichnowsky reported back to von Bethmann-Hollweg an England torn through the centre.

While this melancholy difference was being resolved, it became necessary for the British Fleet to make its ceremonial courtesy visit to the German Naval Review at Kronstadt and Kiel. There, as the month of June moved to a sunlit climax of felicity unknown for years, the great ships of England and of Germany lay moored side by side, their officers and men sharing regattas, banquets, mutual toasts. At a dinner given by the officers of the light cruiser *Southampton* to the German officers a German captain made a speech saying, "War between us would be like civil war." A German officer, unluckily killed in a British seaplane accident, was given a joint funeral of a most moving kind. The Kaiser, in his yacht *Hohenzollern*, sailed through the Kiel Canal, standing alone in his Admiral's uniform on a stage over the upper bridge, while the British crews, well rehearsed, manned ship and cheered.

In the middle of all this, on the 28th June, there came news of an incident far away, a shot fired in a Balkan town remote from all these fraternal celebrations, a tiresome manifestation of that nervous Slavic spirit so incomprehensible to Teutons and Anglo-Saxons alike. The German Emperor was sailing that day in the waters off Kiel. When he heard the news he came instantly ashore; within the hour he had ordered that all his arrangements be cancelled, and that evening he had left Kiel for Berlin. The British fleet moved out, set course for home. It seemed that the Archduke Francis Ferdinand of Austria had been shot and killed in a Serbian township called Sarajevo.

. . . 3

Next day the newspapers said:

> The Archduke Francis Ferdinand, heir to the throne
> of Austro-Hungary, and his morganatic wife, the Duchess
> of Hohenberg, were assassinated yesterday in the town of
> Sarajevo, capital of Bosnia, which was annexed by Austria
> a few years ago. The Royal visit had been in connection
> with certain Army manoeuvres. . . .

It was a piquant item without being especially significant; in most papers it occupied a single-column front-
page top under a thirty-point head—important, by all means,
but scarcely imperative; sudden death is by definition interesting, and more so in the case of minor royalty. If there
should be international implications they would be dynastic
and recondite, possibly even scandalous; there was, after
all, the morganatic wife, and curious anecdotes about the
German Emperor. All this was to emerge in a splendid
flood by and by.

Francis Ferdinand was the eldest son of the Emperor
Franz Josef's brother, the Archduke Karl Ludwig of
Austria-Este, by his second wife Princess Annunciata of

the Two Sicilies: a resounding ancestry. He was born in
1863 at Graz, and most strictly brought up by the Jesuits
under the supervision of his Portuguese stepmother, Maria
Theresa of Braganza. He was not born to inherit a throne.
The Emperor's son Rudolf was the prospective successor,
but on a famous January day of 1889 Rudolf took his life
in the shooting box of Mayerling, in circumstances of romantic tragedy that were by no means to be ignored by
later generations of dramatists and script-writers. Francis
Ferdinand's father was unwilling to claim his rights of
succession, so the young Archduke became heir-presumptive
to the tangled title of Austro-Hungary.

Oddly the strictly clerical, Jesuit-reared Archduke
deviated wildly from protocol in his marriage. The Countess
Sophie Chotek was merely a lady-in-waiting, a daughter
of the former Austrian Minister Plenipotentiary at Dresden,
and when Francis married her he registered his oath on the
Gospels in the presence of the princes and dignitaries of
the realm that he would never seek to endow any sons of the
union with rights to the Crown.

This, in the context of the time, was not without social
interest: it was known that the Countess suffered many in-
dignities, and would absent herself from Court functions
rather than walk at the rear of all processions, behind the
youngest of the debutante Archduchesses. Her husband en-
deavoured to make the position somewhat more tolerable
by bestowing on her the title of Duchess of Hohenberg.
The German Emperor, however, remained friendly; on one
visit by Francis Ferdinand and his wife to Potsdam, the

entire German Royal Family were excluded from the Court entertainments so that the Kaiser might be able to give his arm to the Duchess.

All this compensated in some measure for the cold and professional personality of the Archduke himself, who took his task seriously. He had pensioned off numbers of generals whose birth provided their only title to command and replaced them by expert, if mercenary, soldiers. He had reinforced his Foreign Service by bringing from the Embassy at Saint Petersburg Alois von Aehrenthal, of a Jewish banking family, which marked the first departure of Austrian policies from the defensive position she had observed since the disasters of 1866.

Yet nobody loved him much. It was often recalled, or perhaps invented, that he was with his two brothers when their father the Archduke Karl Ludwig died in 1896, and that the youngest, Ferdinand Karl, threw himself in a passion of grief upon the body; that the second, Otto, hurried to the stables and wept on the neck of his favourite horse— and that Francis Ferdinand opened his father's desk, read the will, and issued orders for the funeral.

He was a chilling personality, yet his own quite casual death was a punctuation-mark in the history of the world.

On that June day the Archduke and his Consort were driving to the town hall of Sarajevo through formally-decorated streets when a Serbian called Cabrinovic, a printer by trade, threw a small bomb at the car. It fell, however, on the folded hood, bounced back on to the road, and exploded behind the second car, slightly injuring Count

Weldeck and Colonel von Merizii, the ADC, and Countess von Lanjus, a lady-in-waiting. Cabrinovic fled, and jumped into the river in an attempt to escape; two policemen leaped in after him and secured him. After some excitement and delay the procession moved on.

On the steps of the town hall, the burgomaster waited, impatient to read his address of welcome. He was dismayed at the unexpected anger of the Archduke, who protested, not unreasonably, that his reception had been "outrageous."

After the ceremony it was suggested that the drive back through the town be abandoned, but the Archduke insisted that he drive to the hospital to see the wounded Colonel von Merizii. On the way there the chauffeur turned by mistake into the narrow Franz Joseph Street, and while he was trying to reverse the car a Serbian called Princip, a student from Grahovo, came close enough to fire two point-blank shots. The first killed the Duchess at once; the second hit the Archduke in the windpipe and he, too, was quickly dead.

The telegrams carried the news like a dark cloud to every Foreign Office in Europe. There were few tears for the Archduke, deep fears for the dynasty. Nothing in the world was more political than the Hapsburg clan; since the collapse of the Holy Roman Empire the Dual Monarchy was something, it was said, that if it did not exist would have to be invented. Austria-Hungary, once bulwark of Europe against the Turks, was still the barricade of Germanism against Slavism—of the Magyars and the Czechs and the Ruthenians and all the other complex South-Eastern Europeans against absorption by the Russians. The 84-year-old Emperor had clearly not long to live; his nearest heir was assassinated; *his* heirs were barred from succession by their morganatic birth—all this in a political mosaic like Austria-Hungary whose dozen or so nationalities were most palpably held together by an Imperial personality and nothing else. Worst of all, he had been murdered in an occupied capital by an irredentist Serb, at precisely the moment, as every diplomatist in Europe knew, when Austria was groping for an anti-Serb issue, and when Germany was awaiting any chance of a reckoning with the Serbs, whom the Kaiser regarded as savages and regicides.

The thing fell like a pall over monarchical Europe, where it was scarcely possible to conceive of any dynastic emergency that was not a family affair. In London the King sent for Sir Douglas Dawson, comptroller of the Lord Chamberlain's Department, to cancel the state ball. Only seven months before, after all, the Archduke and Duchess had been his guests at Windsor. Marlborough House went into mourning at once; Queen Alexandra was entertaining her sister-in-law Queen Olga of Greece, whose husband had himself been assassinated only the previous year. The shadow of the great occupational hazard hung momentarily over the whole network of European royalty.

In Vienna, and in Germany, there were other considerations. Princip's bullet, even as it left the gun on the way to Francis Ferdinand's gullet, had decided the fate of Serbia.

For Austria to move it was necessary to secure the support of Germany; the aged Franz Josef wrote the letter to the Kaiser in his own hand, saying: "I am certain that you also are convinced that any agreement with Serbia is out of the question." A week later the Kaiser wrote back, promising support; perhaps the first genuinely fatal document of the world war that was by then predestined. It was hardly unexpected; eight months earlier the Kaiser had discussed Serbia with Count Berchtold, the Austro-Hungarian Foreign Minister, suggesting the shelling and occupation of Belgrade. "Rest assured," he said, "I stand behind you, and am ready to draw the sword whenever the lead you take makes it necessary."

The Kaiser was due to begin his annual cruise to Scandinavian waters. He was anxious not to arouse suspicion by changing his plans, but before he left he called his Army and Naval chiefs to Potsdam and warned them of what might follow.

It was a good issue, from every point of view. The Serbian issue suited Vienna because it united the Magyars and the Austrian Germans. As a regicide issue it was particularly useful, since it would arouse English prejudices against Serbia. For Berlin it was admirable, as the basic conflict was Austro-Russian, not German-French, and it was much more expedient that Germany should be in a posture of fighting for Austria against a Slav menace than that Austria appear to fight for Germany. As a *casus belli* it could hardly, in the circumstances, be bettered.

And still Austria waited eighteen more days. For Europe there was still a week or two of summer, of commonplace life, of prosperity and peace.

July began in a wave of overpowering heat the like of which had not been recorded for years. The farmers were already seriously alarmed; there had been no real rain since March, most of the root crops were already ruined and the hay harvest was the lightest for years. England was spread with bare and dusty fields.

For three days on end the London thermometers marked 90° in the shade. On one of these days Joseph Chamberlain, ailing for years, quietly died, and there were a few nostalgic obituary recollections of the Boer War and fiscal reform. At Henley for the first time the Americans walked away with the finals; sweating crowds in blazers, tall upright collars, and straw boaters watched Harvard University beat the Union Boating Club of Boston on what was said to be an almost lukewarm Thames.

Uncertain rumours continued to drift in from the Continent. Professor Carl Ballod, writing in the *Preussische Jahrbüche*, suggested that in the event of war the west German industrial population would be faced in a very few weeks with an appalling famine unless a year's grain supply was built up in the urban areas. "The conclusion is interesting," mused the Liberal *Daily News*, "because apparently Germany is no better off in this respect than Free Trade England."

A pamphlet suddenly appeared in Berlin, written by Lieutenant-Colonel Frobenius and recommended by the Crown Prince, called *Germany's Hour of Fate*. It would strike, said the Colonel, in the spring of the following year. It would find the French Army, as now, in a bad way:

with its forts defective in construction, its guns without ammunition and its soldiers without boots. At the same time he noted a marked technical advance in Britain, where the German observers at the Portsmouth naval review itemised with care the new seaplanes on view—"aerial warships," they were called: Bristol tractors, Hewlett-Blondeau BEs, the Sopwith Bat-Boat, Maurice Farman pushers with Renault engines, the Short tractors with 160 horsepower Gnome motors "capable of close on 80 miles an hour."

The most absorbing news from the Continent, however, came as usual from the French courts of justice, which had finally brought themselves to the business of trying the celebrated Madame Caillaux for the most popular murder of the year. Madame Caillaux was the wife of France's ex-Minister of Finance, and in their domestic arrangements they had clearly followed what every Englishman accepted as the true pattern of French family life. The *Figaro* had attacked M. Caillaux by publishing a letter the Minister had written in more than familiar terms to a certain Madame Henriette Rainbouard, signing it "Ton Jo." It announced that it was about to publish two more. Madame Caillaux had thereupon called upon M. Calmette, editor of the *Figaro*, and after an animated conversation had produced a small pistol from her reticule and shot him dead.

The trial was rewardingly emotional, and was followed in close detail in the press. The defence claimed that Madame Caillaux was, despite Madame Rainbouard, a devoted wife, and had intended no more than to teach M. Calmette a sharp lesson; she was therefore handsomely acquitted. It made a brave display in the morning papers. That day 100,000 workers were on strike in Russia; the Cossacks were called into St. Petersburg to crush the riots, and infantry patrolled the Nevsky Prospekt; a brief account of this filled the column below the story of the trial.

That day, too, German security guards picked up a lame man at Friedrichsfeld, near Düsseldorf, and discovered adroitly concealed inside his wooden leg the stolen plans of a nearby fortress, neatly addressed to the French espionage bureau in Geneva.

Westminster was still obsessed with Ireland. To resolve the deadlock, Asquith persuaded King George personally to convene a conference of conciliation at Buckingham Palace under Royal auspices—an unprecedented thing, justified only by the bitter dangers of the day. The King agreed: the conference was called in the Garden Room of the Palace; the King made his speech of welcome and withdrew, leaving the politicians under the chairmanship of Mr. James Lowther, Speaker of the House of Commons.

They held four meetings. Everything broke down on the issue of Tyrone and Fermanagh.

The Speaker was waiting in the anteroom of Buckingham Palace to take his leave of the King. He picked up an evening paper, and the item leaped out of the page: Austria had presented her ultimatum to Serbia.

A few moments later Sir Edward Grey hurried in from the Foreign Office, deeply moved. He had the document in his hand. It was, he said, "unexpectedly severe—harsher in tone and more humiliating in its terms than any communication of which we had recollection addressed by one independent Government to another."

It charged the Serbian Government with neglecting to carry out its undertaking given on 31st March 1909 to "modify the direction of its policy with regard to Austria-Hungary"; it stigmatised as "culpable tolerance" its failure to repress anti-Austrian agitation, and it insisted: (1) that the Serbian Government publish in the Sunday edition of its official organ a condemnation of the anti-Austrian propaganda, an abject apology, and a threat to punish all "anti-Austrian machinations"; (2) that it should suppress all anti-Austrian publications and dissolve the Pan-Serb organisation Narodna Odbrana, (3) dismiss all officers and functionaries "whose names and deeds the Austria-Hungarian Government reserves to itself the right of communicating," and accept the assistance of Austrian agents in so doing, (4) proceed against all accessories to the Sarajevo plot, and deal with all anti-Austrian utterances of Serbian officials, and (5) notify the Austria-Hungarian Government of the execution of these things without delay.

The phraseology was something quite unprecedented even in the brusque context of Balkan affairs. Vienna demanded that Serbia accept these terms by six on the evening of the 25th. There would be no extension of the forty-eight-hour term, and no mediation from any quarter would be in any circumstances acceptable.

Mr. Asquith at once reported to the King: "It is the gravest event for many years past in European politics, as it may be the prelude to a war in which at least four of the Great Powers might be involved. Sir Edward Grey was to suggest to Prince Lichnowsky yesterday evening the possibility of a mediating group, consisting of England, Germany, France, and Italy, offering its services in the interests of peace."

In fact Sir Edward Grey had hesitated over this move, feeling that it was up to some other Power to take the initiative. In any case, he knew, Germany would object to anything in the nature of a court of arbitration. Yet the proposition was just feasible, it might just be done on the lines of the Ambassadors' Conference in 1912–13. The same people were still available in London—Cambon, Lichnowsky, Benckendorff, Imperiali, himself; they were familiar enough with each other. He made the proposal on the Sunday, June 26th, and the Germans reacted as he had foreseen. Grey felt bitterly about the Germans. They had permitted Austria to go too far, letting the feebler ally handle an explosive situation without attempting to moderate her. Germany claimed she had not even seen the ultimatum. Now she rejected this device for a settlement without, as far as Grey could see, even referring it to Austria.

Grey's feelings were despairing. He knew that war would be a disastrous thing not only in degree but in kind. In the past, warring nations had released their manpower and resources only in fractions and driblets, now it must be inevitably in a flood. Old wars had been more manageable; at least it had been easier to distinguish the spheres of Army and politics, whereas today, since the Curragh affair the Army was intervening in politics in a fashion never seen since Cromwell. Every problem would be multiplied and new ones born for a nation that had not fought a major war since Waterloo. Mass armies, total effort, industrial concentration, civilian morale. . . . Yet Grey knew he must support France and he knew what intense opposition he would face in Cabinet. He was almost ready to resign.

But time was wasting fast; on that Sunday Austria began to mobilise.

From that evening the Cabinet met daily, often twice daily.

It chanced that Prince Henry of Prussia, the Kaiser's brother, had been yachting at Cowes. He hurried to Buckingham Palace to say goodbye to his cousin, King George. When he reached Kiel two days later he wrote to the Kaiser, quoting the King who, he said, had told him: "We shall try all we can to keep out of this and remain neutral." The Kaiser took this at its face value, and was soon afterwards to requote it urgently in a telegram to President Wilson as evidence that he had King George's word on Britain's neutrality. The statement was firmly denied. No record whatever of the conversation remains, said the Palace.

The days were full of such cross-purposes.

During those hanging two days after the ultimatum it began increasingly to be felt that the only possible way of avoiding war was for Serbia to submit. Austria's demands, it was argued, were certainly arrogant, but not indeed intolerable, in view of the provocation; when the terms were stripped of their needlessly aggressive language they were only what any state had the natural right to demand of another. Nobody in Britain, to be sure, was in any way pro-Serbian either intellectually or emotionally. To the few who ever considered the matter at all, Serbia was a state with which Britain had been compelled to break diplomatically a few years before after the brutal murder of the King and Queen; the quarrel had been patched up, but without any kind of sentimental conciliation. Serbia was a faraway country, of which one knew little.

On Tuesday June 28th the German naval attaché in London wired Berlin:

> British Second Fleet fully manned, First Fleet reported at Portland, one submarine flotilla left Portsmouth. Battleship Bellerophon on way to Gibraltar for refit, recalled. Ships of Second and Third Fleet have coaled and armed. Great dockyard activity. Movements of ships no longer published.

Winston Churchill had been First Lord of the Admiralty for three years. In his room at the Admiralty he maintained a great map on which, every day of those three years, he caused the position of the German Fleet to be marked. He was eager, exuberant, restless, ingenious, determined. Many Liberals mistrusted him as a renegade Tory; all Tories mistrusted him as an impulsive firebrand. He now sent a minute to Prince Louis of Battenberg, First

Sea Lord: "Collect minesweepers. All vessels on Irish coast to be ready for mobilisation. Triumph to close the China flagship. Report positions of aircraft in Thames estuary."

Already Mr Churchill was impatient to get the Fleet to war stations, and to do so through the Channel, so that the South Coast should not be left unguarded. He decided not to consult the Cabinet, which in its immensely touchy mood would have certainly considered the move provocative. He told the Prime Minister and secured his agreement, and on Wednesday June 29th the Fleet steamed out of Portland, through the dark of night, without lights, on a mid-Channel course through the Straits. By next day they were well into the North Sea.

That evening the German Ambassador complained bitterly about this to Sir Edward Grey. Grey assured him wanly that the move had no aggressive intention; the ships were in no way approaching German ports. But Mr Churchill noted that the ships were now in good position. They could no longer be held in port. They were mobile; they could vanish at command; they were ready. Mr Churchill glowed.

By now the machine seemed to be grinding irresistibly on. Serbia—as everyone had expected and on the whole, indeed, hoped—caved in; even so her reply to the Austrians was notably conciliatory. She accepted the ultimatum on almost every point; she offered to refer every aspect of the dispute to the Hague Tribunal; she would collaborate with Austria's agents in uncovering the Sarajevo plot—but she would not countenance the activities of Austrian agents inside Serbia.

The reply was instantly, and inevitably, rejected as insufficient. On 25th July the Dual Monarchy withdrew its representative from Belgrade. The following day Mr Jovanovic, the Serbian Ambassador in Vienna, was handed his passport.

The curious thing is that only then did the desperation of the crisis begin to leak into the British newspapers, and even at this stage the headlines were no more than "Serbian War Scare." The distractions at home were still considerable: that very day troops in Dublin had fired on the crowds, killing four people, including a woman and a small boy, and wounding thirty more.

At Olympia there was a fight for the World Heavy-weight Championship, in which the twenty-year-old Georges Carpentier beat Britain's Gunboat Smith, who was disqualified in the sixth round, having somehow contrived to punch the Frenchman on the head while he was down.

The King cancelled his visit to Goodwood. Sir Arthur Nicolson, Permanent Under-Secretary at the Foreign Office, called on the Austrian and Russian Embassies, and was himself called on by the French Ambassador. Sir Francis Bertie, British Ambassador in Paris, and Sir Edward Goschen, in Berlin, hastened back from London to their posts. The diplomatic world began to hum and vibrate like a beehive.

The position of Britain depended entirely on her posture in relation to the Triple Alliance, and already the leader-writers were beginning to define and simplify this in easy terms. Under the Triple Alliance, if Austria-Hungary or Germany was attacked by Russia, each was bound to go to the aid of the one attacked. If Austria-Hungary or Germany was attacked by anyone other than Russia, the second partner was to preserve a benevolent neutrality. If Austria-Hungary or Germany attacked Russia, neither was under any obligation to help the attacking power. The nature of Italy's obligations was uncertain; they were presumed to be chiefly towards Germany, providing for mutual assistance in the event of an attack by, but not on, France.

Under the Dual Alliance, if Russia or France was attacked by a third power, whether Germany or any other, the partner was obliged to go to the help of the attacked state. If either of them themselves attacked a third power, there was no mutual obligation of any kind.

Britain was technically bound by no treaty with any of the partners, and was generally held to be free to decide any case on its proper merits. Nine years before, to be sure, at the time of the Moroccan conflict between France and Germany, the French had spoken of a promise by Britain to throw a force of 150,000 men into the Continent if required. But only a year ago, in 1913, Mr Asquith had declared: "This country is not under any obligation not public and known to Parliament which compels it to take part in any war. In other words, if war comes between European Powers there are no unpublished agreements which will restrict the freedom of the Government or Parliament to decide whether or not Great Britain should participate in a war."

This, it was pointed out, did not include and made no reference to moral undertakings: the great imponderables.

4

By now Britain, the country that had forgotten what war was, had been shocked into accepting it at least as a conceivable possibility; the experience was disruptive. The newspapers' wildly contending attitudes for once reflected the immense differences that had split the nation, that had disturbed Parliament, that had divided the Cabinet itself. Nobody was "for" the war, or cared at least to be expressly held to be so, and great numbers were urgently and articulately against it. True, much of the Tory press was loudly and emotionally indignant against Germany on simple principle; those were the days when *Punch* was incomplete without a taunt against "the Teutons"—whoever they might be—or an imaginative drawing of some Prussian invasion. "Saki" had written a novel the previous year in which the Kaiser, having subdued England, was vanquished by a troop of Boy Scouts. Strange stories suddenly swept through southern England of mysterious airships hovering over the East Coast. The *Daily Mail* raised a great campaign for the appointment of an Air Minister—of all unheard-of things—and for a British fleet of dirigibles. The paper promoted a big public rally at the Mansion House to demand these bizarre innovations.

Nevertheless in Parliament at least three-quarters of the members were still determined not to be drawn into any sort of war unless the United Kingdom was attacked, a consideration that seemed impossibly unlikely. Bismarck had said, the year before he died, "The great European war could come out of some damned foolish thing in the Balkans." It seemed now that the old man could indeed have been right. Everything depended on the Czar. What would he do if Austria insisted on wreaking a physical vengeance on Serbia? That question raised others: Could Austria conscientiously invade a country that had virtually abased herself by accepting the ultimatum? And if she did, would Russia march against Austria? If so, would Germany take arms against Russia? Would France then march against Germany? There the chain of reactions led hopelessly and inescapably to Britain's door. In the event of all these aberrations, would England then support France?

In the lobbies the arguments were furious. Since Serbia had cringed, Austria would not attack—or if she did, Russia would stay out; or if Russia came in Germany would not; or if Germany did move on Russia, France and Germany would cancel each other out. It was unthinkable that Germany should go through Belgium—or if she did, Belgium would not resist. Perhaps Belgium had a secret agreement with Germany to allow the passage of her troops; anything was possible. Belgium, after all, had asked from England neither help nor guarantees (nor indeed did she until August 3rd, the very eve of Britain's entry in the war).

As for France: if France became involved it would not be because it was her quarrel but because, as Russia's ally, she had had the folly and bad luck to become involved in Russia's feuds. What, one asked, would be the advantage of a British national policy that had so scrupulously and successfully avoided European commitments and entanglements if one was to blunder into a disaster of this kind? Both sides of the House agreed among themselves that there was enough national opinion to bring down the Government; public support, it was said, could never possibly be raised for any war supporting Russia in her quarrel with Austria over Serbia.

What was Serbia anyhow? One undefinable and historically distasteful unit in an endemically turbulent and quarrelsome section of Europe's most ungovernable quarter. What, if it came to that, was France? Frivolity and license, with a social quality adapted only for abandoned recreation and sensual pleasure—brave, no doubt, in a romantic way, but politically dubious and unstable. Germany was beer and bands; no more. And Russia—Russians were barely humans, groping in an obscure freezing fog of tyranny and ignorance. They had been defeated in the Far East by the infinitely more efficient and resourceful Japanese. Where was any obligation or advantage that made sense to practical men to interrupt the peace of Britain for any such considerations?

In 1914, after all, Britain was the richest and most

prosperous nation in Europe. She had enormous invest-
ments in North and South America, in Asia, in most of
the countries of Europe. To remain neutral would be to
preserve them all, doubtless to enhance them. To fight—
with no guarantee of national survival, let alone certain
victory—would be to hazard everything that had been
built on a century of industrious, solid, successful, admirable commercial adventure.

The emergency pointed up all the mutual suspicions
in the House—the Conservatives believed the Liberals to
be spoiled pacifists at heart, Little Englanders; they feared
Asquith's men would use a war as an excuse to introduce
any number of their hoarded measures: extension of the
franchise, social reforms of absurd kinds, even prohibition.
The Liberals feared that the Tories would exploit the emotion inevitably aroused by war for nationalist and imperialist ends.

Against all this was Sir Edward Grey and his conscience. Grey's political certainties, developed through the
years of diplomatic catch-as-catch-can, were now in dire
conflict with his moral self. Until the very last moment
Sir Edward Grey, the patriotic Whig, deeply believed that
the glaring immensity of the danger would itself avert it;
the fact that the war would be so unprecedentedly catastrophic would be so obvious to the Powers that they must
recoil from it. Grey had better reason than most to be
conscious of the long pattern of expedients and duplicities,
the years of diplomatic bargaining and bribery, the cynical
political horse-trading of the Balkan complex, the network

of secret factors that now seemed about to engulf the Continent. Yet even he could not emotionally reconcile himself to its logical end—to the end of the Liberal dream of universal enlightenment and goodwill, the end of security, the end of expansive living, of insularity; indeed the end of peace. Also in his heart he knew the changes that would be precipitated in the established and proper order of life. He foresaw a terrible set of social forces certain to be released, to drive through the pleasant world he knew and that his kind had always known. In the end, whatever the end might be, all Europe's populations would not reflect to adjudicate on particular national responsibilities for the war, which, as God and Grey knew, were historically doubtful; even if they did, they would insist that wherever lay the particular guilt, the system that produced it was vulnerable and venal, and must be changed. Throughout the last days this intolerable dilemma obsessed him. When it was too late to stop the inevitable he said to Count Mensdorff, the Austrian Ambassador, "I hate it, I hate it!" And impulsively he added that if Russia had been the first to attack he, Edward Grey, would have been prepared to stand by Germany. The consequences of the war would be terrible, he said: "It is the greatest step towards Socialism that could have been made. We shall have Labour Governments in every country after this." And indeed he was not far wrong; after the war Russia had her Revolution and Germany her Republic, Italy changed her whole political system, Austria-Hungary vanished from the map, and by and by Britain, too, had the Labour Government that had haunted the Secretary of State for so long.

Grey's conscience was given no peace. It was assailed on one side by Sir Eyre Crowe, who insisted that we had to support the French "as an honourable expectation had been raised" which we could not repudiate. It was harried by Mr Gwynne in the Tory *Morning Post*. It was tormented by the daily interviews, each one more distressing, with M. Cambon, the French Ambassador. Britain, urged M. Cambon, with a sort of controlled desperation, had never experienced an 1870. Britain was an island—but how long, demanded the Ambassador, could this last?

By now Bonar Law was conferring with Grey every day. If the Liberals were torn with uncertainties so were the Conservatives; there was no real unanimity even on the Right. The Cabinet, said Bonar Law, was in no position to pledge the country on an issue of this kind—the only general concession of the Opposition could be to approve His Majesty's Government in their efforts to initiate negotiations for a European settlement. It approved the warning messages sent on 27th July to the Dominions and Colonies, and the next day's alert-signals to the Navy and Army. The Cabinet members were willing that Germany should be told firmly not to rely upon British neutrality, but the majority strongly opposed giving M. Cambon the assurances and guarantees for which he was now pleading several times a day.

To the end of that confused July many Liberals continued to argue that the best way of resisting war was most scrupulously not to invite it. Thanks to Fisher, England had the new all-big-gun Dreadnought battleship. (Although the Liberals in their first three years of office had cut down the building programme by a third, feeling the money could be better spent by Lloyd George, nevertheless after pressure the Navy had been allotted its eight battleships.)

On July 28th the Austro-Hungarian Empire declared war on Serbia. It was solemn and formal; there were to be many such declarations in the next few days.

Count von Berchtold, Austrian Foreign Minister, announced: "The Royal Government of Serbia not having given a satisfactory reply to the Note presented to it by the Austria-Hungarian Minister in Belgrade on July 23rd 1914, the Imperial and Royal Government of Austria-Hungary finds it necessary to safeguard its rights and interests and to have recourse for this purpose to force of arms. Austria-Hungary therefore considers itself from this moment in a state of war with Serbia."

Only now, at last, the situation forced itself on the attention of Fleet Street; at last the story led the British papers.

The Serbian Legation in London reacted with a baffling euphoria, an optimism in the circumstances almost fey.

"Of course Russia will rush to our aid!" declared the attaché in London, M. Woislav Petrovic. "And Russia, fresh from her experience with Japan, will be striking at the happiest psychological moment. Russia is our dear brother, and we are bent upon fulfilling the dream of Napoleon, and working towards a Slav Empire. A United States of Slavdom!" he cried. "There are one hundred and eighty millions of us!"

He suddenly relapsed into bitterness. "Why should Belgrade be held responsible for the Sarajevo assassination?" he demanded. "Did not an Italian, Luigi Lucani, murder the Empress Elisabeth? Was Rome responsible for that? Another Italian killed President McKinley—was Italy to blame?"

But already he was rationalising something long past reason. That evening the first shells fell on Belgrade.

Clearly the first community in London to take fright was the City, by now in a condition of near demoralisation. Wildly alarmed lest the public should lose its own head and jettison its stock, dealers marked down prices as had never been done before. Consols opened at 74⅜ on July 25th, compared with Friday's closing price of 75. It was no time at all before the world's premier security dropped as low as 73¼—a loss on the day of 1¾. Only a little time before a fall in Consols of ½ caused gruesome shivers up every back in Lombard Street.

A possibly disastrous panic was averted by the knowledge that the speculative account open was infinitesimal anyway—there had been no speculative initiative on the Stock Exchange for years; the boom in industry had been absorbing too much money, leaving little for adventure. Moreover the series of turbulent financial and political developments all over the world—in Brazil, Canada, Mexico, Ulster—had sent people back to the stocking instead of the stocks.

Business could still be done in small quantities, on what would ordinarily have been considered impossible terms. The great object in view was to keep resources as liquid —in money form—as possible, in case things got worse. In the money market some houses refused to discount bills at all; others reluctantly accepted a few at much higher than the Bank Rate. All over Europe the Bourses were rocking, and in Paris there was a sensational run on the Bank of France, where a queue two miles long gathered at four in the morning to change notes for gold.

It was worse than horrifying; it was unorthodox. "If the effect of a localised war is so serious," wrote the *Daily News* city editor, "one is driven furiously to think what would happen in the event of a 'great' European war. It is disturbing even to reflect on the matter."

It was pointed out that other wars had been between nations generally self-sustaining; the modern world of 1914 was built on such an intricate and interlocking system of credits and commerce that it had virtually become a single entity.

On 31st July the London Stock Exchange closed on a business day for the first time in its history.

The Bank Rate doubled, from 4% to 8%.

All over Britain the citizens besieged the banks to draw out sovereigns.

It was, after all, Bank Holiday eve.

On the last day but one of the last month of European peace, within one step of the first total war, Mr Asquith was in the Cabinet room, still studying the map of Ulster, buried in official statistics on proportionate populations and religions, preparing his speech for the forthcoming Amending Bill. For the Prime Minister, a man of almost inhuman powers of concentration, there was at that moment still no

Serbia, no Austria, no Berlin, no Saint Petersburg: only Ireland.

In the middle of this academic consideration came a telephone call from Bonar Law, urging the Prime Minister at all costs to arrange an immediate rendezvous with him and Carson. They met, and agreed that the second reading of the Amending Bill should be postponed; it would be grave folly at such a time to advertise their political dissension to the world.

Asquith hurried back to consult Grey and Lloyd George; they decided they must close with the offer.

"The City," wrote Asquith in his journal, "is in a terrible state of depression and paralysis, and for the time being all against intervention. The prospect is very black."

Later that day, July 30th, the full Cabinet met to review in detail whatever British obligations there might be in respect of the neutrality of Belgium under the Treaties of 1839. There were differences of opinion on how deeply a single guaranteeing state was bound to maintain Belgium's neutrality if the other contracting states refused or abstained. It was finally held to be a matter of policy rather than a moral obligation. The Cabinet decided that Grey should inform the German and French embassies that Britain was at that stage unable to pledge herself in advance either in all conditions to stand aside or in any conditions to join in.

That afternoon Goschen wired to Grey from Berlin that he had seen the German Chancellor, who had told him that while he believed the principle guiding British policy was not to stand aside if France were crushed, that was in no way Germany's intention. If he could be assured of Britain's neutrality, said the Chancellor, Germany would formally guarantee to acquire no territory at the expense of France. Goschen had then asked if this applied also to France's colonies, but the Chancellor had not felt able to give a similar undertaking there.

Clearly, then, Bethmann-Hollweg believed war to be not only likely but imminent. Grey replied at once instructing Goschen to say that His Majesty's Government could not possibly entertain such a proposal, that Britain would never bind herself to non-belligerency on such equivocal terms—to stand by if France were beaten and her colonies seized, so long as no "French territory" was absorbed. His Majesty's Government, wrote Sir Edward Grey wearily, would reserve the right to act as circumstances seemed to require.

> There is in our midst [said the *Manchester Guardian* on 1st August] a grim conspiracy to force us into the war should the attempts of the peacemakers fail. The objects of the conspirators are now openly avowed. We are to join in, not under certain conditions or in defence of this or that British interest, but in any case.
>
> We are to do this for three reasons. The first is that we are bound in our own interests to maintain the balance of power in Europe. The second is that we are protectors of the neutrality of Belgium. The balance of power, as a doctrine of English policy, was responsible for the long feud with France in the 18th Century, culminating in the war with Revolutionary France. It made the National

Debt. It lost England the great lead it had obtained in constitutional liberties. . . . Its revival has been the work of the last seven or eight years and, we deeply regret to think, has been coincident with the access to power of the Liberal Government. . . .

Even if we admired the system as much as we in fact detest it, it supplies no reason why we should take the side of Russia against Germany. If Russia wins, there will be the greatest disturbance of the balance of power ever seen. The whole condition of our existence as an Asiatic power will have to be revised. . . . The victory of Germany on the other hand, would in effect be a victory for the principle of the balance of power. If we believed in this principle—which we do not—we might be for intervention on the side of Germany. Because we do not believe in it we are able without the least misgiving to counsel neutrality.

That day the Waxwork Exhibition of Madame Tussaud, in Baker Street, rushed a new Scena entitled "The Crisis of Europe, with Lifelike Portrait Models of King George, the Emperor of Austria, King Peter of Serbia, and Other Reigning Sovereigns."

The country was, unarguably, on the edge of war; under another constitution it would possibly have been already at the barricades. Asquith called it "A Time of Gravity almost unparalleled in the experience of anyone." The imminence of danger turned all manner of arguments and disputes inwards to the technique of politics at such a time: how could a divided administration of a divided country declare a war and commit a nation to something it had no means of understanding?

The British system of government had been defined simply as a Cabinet dictatorship limited by quinquennial elections, and these after all could be described as only a general judgment on the comparative merits of the existing Government and the Opposition in the most general terms; there was no question of adjudicating on special issues, individual policies. In any case, as everyone knew, the value of that sanction varied enormously according to how near such an election happened to be. This system, wholly illogical and potentially perilous in theory, was held to have been somehow or other modified over the years by an ingrown pattern of checks and balances—impossible to define, in the last resort, since there was no method of writing them into a constitution that was itself unwritten. A Cabinet was bound to be controlled by questions of personal conscience on the one hand and the possibility of Parliamentary defeat on the other—still, the last time a Government with a clear Parliamentary majority had been brought down by a House of Commons vote in time of peace had been nineteen years before, in 1895, when Rosebery resigned and Salisbury succeeded—and that had been followed by the Ashanti Expedition and the Jameson Raid.

Often in the days to come Asquith was to be criticised in the light of what did happen: he should have rationalised the Entente into a firm Alliance and raised a conscript army to implement it; alternatively he should have formally disentangled himself from the shapeless Franco-Russian association and announced Britain's inevitable neutrality. But for the first it would have been necessary to work with almost sinister finesse upon a party by nature pacific, that would strongly oppose the militarisation of funds designed for social reform. It would have been imperative to create a picture of a Germany potentially hostile and menacing and thus, he could argue, building up a psychological atmosphere in which Germany must actually become hostile. As for the second—Mr Asquith, too, had his scruples.

By now the press had aligned itself firmly on each side of the fence. The Tory press was eagerly and angrily demanding war; the Northcliffe group—which included not only the *Daily Mail* and the *Evening News*, but also the *Times*—enthusiastically accepted the reborn name of Jingoes. Loudly they raised their voices against the great murmuring that opposed a possible war, expressed by the Liberal press, especially the *Daily News*.

> With credit gone [said the *News* at the end of July] business must come to a standstill; mills, factories, workshops must close down; and if war follows on the threat of war, food will go up to famine prices. Within a few days of England launching into this struggle the streets of every English town will be filled with starving men, women, and children, who either have no money because there is no work or whose wages under the blast of famine can no longer keep body and soul together. . . .
>
> Supposing we follow the counsel of the Jingoes and join in with France and Russia? Two consequences may follow—either the Russo-Franco-British combination wins, or it is defeated. If it is defeated then not only will hosts of English lives have been sacrificed and millions of English homes ruined, but we shall have smashed the Empire.

If the Russo-Franco-British combination were to win, we shall have gained nothing. Russia and France would partition Germany, and Russia would dominate Europe. The balance of power would be irretrievably, eternally overthrown to make Russia dictator. Who can doubt that after we had helped Russia to destroy Germany and planted her firmly in the seat of supremacy she would turn against us and seize Persia and India? This is the madness and the infamy to which those who talk of our "honour" and the sacred cause of the balance of power are inviting us. Gambling is one thing, but a throw of the dice when nothing can be won and everything lost is insanity.

This was by no means a singular attitude. Individual and collective demands for a policy of neutrality were published by Gilbert Murray, G. M. Trevelyan, Hall Caine, Josiah Wedgwood, Thomas Hardy, Norman Angell, George Lansbury, Cunninghame Graham, Arthur Henderson. An immense meeting in Trafalgar Square was organised by the International Labour Bureau in favour of British neutrality. It was addressed by Keir Hardie himself, the fervent and still beloved Socialist pioneer, who cried: "If there is one country with which England ought not to have any agreement it is the foul Government of anti-democratic Russia!"

A letter was sent to all the press signed by fifty Professors and Fellows of Cambridge University, saying: "No vital interest of this country is endangered such as would justify our participation in a war."

Manifestoes on the same lines were issued by the Lord Mayor of Manchester, the Lord Provost of Glasgow, the

Bishop of Lincoln, the Bishop of Hereford, Professor Sir J. J. Thomson, Sir Lou Mather.

A. G. Gardiner wrote a flaming article in which he described the Czar as

> . . . a weak man, superstitious, under the influence now of inhuman philosophers like Pobiedonostseff or Meshkershtsky, now of mystics and charlatans like Philippe and Rasputin, who decorates his Black Hundred on the morrow of their massacres and holds half Europe in the grip of a mediaeval despotism.
>
> Why, he demanded, is a European war threatened to save Serbia from punishment? Because Serbia is the instrument of Russia. It is through Belgrade that Russia hopes to establish her domination of the Balkan peninsula. . . .

At midnight on 30th July the Czar of All the Russias ordered the already half-completed mobilisation to extend to the entire Army.

In London the Privy Council approved a communiqué to be issued by the War Office: "The military movements which have taken place in Britain are of a purely precautionary nature. In accordance with the ordinary routine, when precautionary measures are put into force, the Special Reserve Sections of the Territorial Force are being employed, members of these sections being under an agreement in accordance with the terms of Section XIII (2) (b) of the Territorial and Reserve Forces Act 1907 to serve in such cases . . ."

A proclamation prohibited the export of "war and certain other materials."

The public, which until a few days before had given every evidence of unawareness of the accelerating crisis, reacted with the inevitable reflex of householders faced with emergency: they rushed the food-shops. So many stores and warehouses were themselves taken by surprise that stocks melted away, emphasising the process, and so rapidly was completed the chain-reaction of demand-scarcity-demand that the Government hurriedly issued an official tranquilizer. There was no need for panic, insisted the statement; the previous week the United Kingdom had received 30,000 hundredweight of Russian and Serbian butter—about twenty per cent of the usual imported supply. The Chilean and Argentine wheat harvest was on its way. "We have," said the Government, "the entire American Continent to draw upon." For a while the demand subsided; Bank Holiday approached, under turquoise skies and a tranquil sun.

5

In Paris too that summer had been singularly sweet and care-free; it was to be remembered for a generation, sometimes with a nearly unbearable nostalgia, as tinged with a special gaiety and delight, for once full of hope and not disen-chantment. The peculiar splendour of the weather rein-forced the old pleasures and stimulated the new—the *bateaux mouches* slid twinkling round the islands of the Seine; the children gathered to the *petits guignols* of the Luxembourg Gardens, their fathers to the bar of the Bal Tabarin or the *promenoir* of the Folies Bergère, in those days still fre-quented even by Parisians. The English language, in all its variants, was everywhere, carrying with it the promise of tourist lavishness. There was modish prosperity for the Houses of Worth and of Poiret, intellectual adventure on the Left Bank among the *Fauves*, or among the curious Post-Impressionists in the gallery of Ambroise Vollard. By all means there seemed to be trouble and unrest abroad, the Balkans were full of disturbing clouds, but as everyone knew this was part of the elaborate machinery by which politi-cians sustained themselves, compelling a fretful interest in their interminably tedious profession. The serious disputes were over contentious tendencies like "Cubism" or "Futurism," over dangerous innovations like Stravinsky's brutal *Sacre du Printemps*, a matter full of far richer controversy. Until, of course, there burst the even more gross and immediate controversy, between the distracted Princip and the Austrian Archduke at Sarajevo. Even among the greater preoccupations it could hardly be ignored.

Outside the coteries, France was suddenly paralysed with dismay. Could this sort of thing be possible *again?* Was not such a prospect manifestly insane, when there was so much to do elsewhere and otherwise? So many of the French still personally remembered the siege of Paris; the starvation, the hopelessness, the degradation of everything; this could not conceivably happen again, not even for Alsace-Lorraine.

The Quai d'Orsay filed the intelligence that Germany was preparing; the last four classes released from the colours had been put in readiness; the requisitions had begun; in the Grand Duchy of Baden all automobiles had already been put at the disposition of the Army.

The French Army stopped all furloughs. A press curtain was pulled down on all military movement. The hoarding of food began—the inevitable peasant reflex to all moments of danger.

The curious fact is that all this time the President of the Republic, M. Poincaré, and the Prime Minister-plus-Foreign Minister M. Viviani, had been on an official visit to Russia. The ceremonies were abruptly cancelled; the Ministers returned hurriedly by battleship. They arrived back in Paris on 29th July—the squat and square Poincaré, the Lorrainer; Viviani with the awkward shambling gait, the materialist anticlerical peaceful man with the golden voice. They were met at the station by great crowds singing "La Marseillaise."

That was the day the Serbian Army blew the bridge between Semlin and Belgrade.

The French Cabinet issued an immediate order to the War Office: no troops were to be stationed within ten kilometres of the German border; those already there were to be withdrawn. Almost did the Government give the impression, in those last days, of inviting attack, so earnest was the intention not to appear even remotely responsible for anything that might occur. Joffre, the Commander-in-Chief, protested; the prohibited zone included precisely those positions a German Army could most easily take. On the very day before war began, the Government restored him liberty to move his troops where he would; nevertheless Joffre did not at once order the arming of the frontier, saying: "If there are to be incidents, they must arise on French territory; let the world see it."

On 31st July all telegraph wires were cut on the German side. The railway was cut at Pagny: all frontier traffic came to a stop. The news surged through the country that both Austria-Hungary and Russia had mobilised. And Germany—Germany herself, the neighbour enemy, the one historic threat—that day issued a proclamation of *Kriegsgefahr:* the State of War. This was not martial law, to be sure, but it was a dire emergency measure, giving the military authorities control over transport, communications, all public services of every kind.

France mobilised the "G.V.C."—the *Gardes des Voies et Communications,* the force of home guards who were said to live on level crossings.

Over Paris the sun still shone, brilliantly, ironically; but between it and the city below had already drifted the blackening cloud of doubt that became unrest, that became first apprehension and then fear and at last a kind of resigned desperation, haunted by the sense of *déjà vu.* Outside the Government offices stretched long queues of Germans and Austrians applying for their papers to return home, arguing through the *guichets,* pressing against the unshakeable barriers of French officialdom. The Parisians watched them glumly. There were no demonstrations. Nothing had happened yet; the world might yet continue.

"*Les temps où nous vivons,*" wrote Guillaume Apollinaire, "*sont si faits pour mourir.*" On that last day of July Paris rocked to an even more immediate drama: Jean Jaurès was murdered.

Nothing, at that moment, could have been more startling and symbolic. Jean Jaurès, the great Socialist, the great orator, the physical expression of French intellectual radicalism, publicly detested as only the French can detest their idols and admired as only the French can admire their iconoclasts—that he should die brought the black cloud down to the rooftops.

Jean Jaurès had spent his life warring on capitalism, defending the policies of Revisionism. He was lucid and passionate and individualist and heterodox and beloved; he was still articulately opposed to doctrinaire Marxism, insisting that the regeneration of society must come on a collective basis, and gradually. He was said by his friends to be a man so kind and merciful that he would denounce and destroy all those who were not; that he loved peace so deeply that he would fight for it to the death.

He had returned only the day before from Brussels, where he had been addressing an anti-war demonstration of the International Socialist Bureau, and that day he was sitting in the Café du Croissant, on the rue Montmartre, just round the corner from the office of *Humanité*, of which he was political director, talking with Jean Longuet, of the "Huma" staff. He had his back to the open ground-floor window against which the curtains were drawn. A young man with a gun clambered on the window-sill and fired two shots from the range of a few feet. Jean Jaurès, hit on each side of the neck, rose briefly to his feet, then his knees collapsed and he sank slowly underneath the table, and presently died.

When they seized the assassin, he said he had killed Jean Jaurès for opposing the Three Years Military Service Act. He had erased all identifications from his clothes, but soon it was learned that he was a student from the Louvre Art School, son of a Rheims registrar called Vilain. He meant little in time to come, just as Princip of Sarajevo meant little in time to come.

For a while the death of Jean Jaurès was a greater

Parisian sensation than the imminence of war itself. He had an immense funeral, with crowds so great that the Government, alarmed, held back the 2nd Regiment of Cuirassiers that was entraining for the border. At the head of the huge procession were carried the Red Flags—and at the rear followed the conservatives and the Clericals.

His last recorded words were those of his Brussels speech the previous day:

> I have never hesitated to invoke on my head the hatred of the Chauvinists. Our rulers are hesitating. Let us profit by this and organise ourselves. The French Government is the best ally for peace of the admirable British Government, which has taken the initiative in the matter of conciliation, and which is giving Russia counsels of prudence and patience. If Russia should take no notice, then it is our duty to declare: We know only one treaty —the treaty that binds us to humanity.

It seemed to precipitate everything that was waiting to be done. The next day at half-past five in the afternoon the mobilisation notices dropped through the letter-boxes in every arrondissement of Paris, every department of the nation; throughout the Republic of France men read them, cursed, shrugged, prayed, blasphemed, and reported to the Commissaries; to this country above all war was hateful, odious, disrupting, inevitable—and near at hand.

The shops closed, and the sun continued to shine. It was war after all. Until yesterday it had been suspense, rancour, indecision, uncertainty. Now a man could capitulate, hand over his emotions and his initiative, obey orders.

In a nation of conscription the dilemma was resolved. The certainty of war meant a kind of peace. The anguish endured, but the problem was gone.

One question remained: What would the English do? Obviously, nothing. It would, once again, be a matter of *perfide Albion,* the fair-weather friend—or, supposing she were driven to intervention by the remnants of a conscience or self-interested fear, where was her Army, where was her compulsory service? Was there such a thing as an English patriotism capable of surviving a cross-Channel journey? By God's grace there was always Russia. . . .

As Jean Jaurès lay dying that Friday in the rue Montmartre, in London Sir Edward Grey wired formal diplomatic approaches to the governments of France and Germany for assurances that they had no intention of violating the sovereign neutrality of Belgium.

France naturally agreed without hesitation and almost without qualification. Sir Francis Bertie telegraphed back from the British Embassy in Paris:

> French Government resolved to respect the neutrality of Belgium. Only in the event of some other Power violating that neutrality that France might be under the necessity of acting otherwise in defence of her own security.

From the British Embassy in Berlin, Sir Edward Goschen advised Grey:

> I have seen the Secretary of State who informs me he must consult the Emperor and the Chancellor before he

could possibly answer. I gathered from what he said that he thought any reply they might give could not but disclose a certain amount of their plan of campaign in the event of war ensuing, and he was therefore very doubtful whether they would return any answer at all. It appears from what he said that the German Government consider that certain hostile acts have already been committed by Belgium. As an instance of this, he alleged that a consignment of corn destined for Germany had been placed under an embargo already.

So, it seemed, had almost everything else in the Low Countries. In London the management of the South Eastern and Chatham Railway had a telegram from their agent in Flushing: all trains from Flushing to Cologne and South Germany had been cancelled. Belgium stopped all railway traffic whatever to Germany. Both she and Holland were under mobilisation orders; all Europe was beginning to echo to the thud of the military tread.

The Foreign Office in Whitehall issued a statement that no concern should be felt for those British citizens who were still abroad; they were in no danger, though "it is possible they may be put to some inconvenience."

The profundity of that understatement could be proved every moment of the twenty-four hours in the Channel ports, in which the tourists, rushing out of France as from a trap, were collecting in surging and desperate bottlenecks. The confusion in Calais was sensational; in the station it was almost impossible to move at all. Nearly two thousand travellers had piled up, awaiting the Channel packet, unwashed, unshaven, struggling amongst themselves in terrible frustrations seeking their possessions in mountains of unsorted luggage. The management of the station buffet had resourcefully stacked the counters with mountains of sandwiches and gallons of coffee awaiting the afternoon train from Paris, which was expected to be the last. Along the Calais sidings stood rows of Belgian loco-motives, suddenly run out of Belgium in panic.

In Paris itself the scene was reproduced; for the first time for many years the great iron gates of the Gare du Nord were closed, while the crowds of all nationalities milled and contended inside. No one could reach the ticket *guichets;* it made no difference, for no one was able to check the tickets. Through the crowds weaved erratic lines of French infantrymen, loaded and caparisoned like White Knights with newly-drawn equipment and all the random clanking miscellaneous gear of the *poilu.*

That day, from the South West India Dock on the London River, a handful of people gathered to watch a small ship sail: the *Endurance,* carrying Sir Ernest Shackle-ton to the Antarctic.

That day, too, the French chefs of the House of Com-mons were sent back to France to join their colours.

On the first day of August, which was Saturday, in Downing Street Mr Asquith called his Private Secretary, Sir Maurice Bonham-Carter, and Sir William Tyrrell to draft a personal communication from King George V to the Czar. Then he called a taxicab and drove with Tyrrell to Buckingham Palace. They arrived at one thirty in the morning and aroused the King, who emerged from his bed in his dressing-gown, to initial the message. Then the Prime Minister returned dutifully to write up his diary. "Winston very bellicose," he wrote, "demanding instant mobilisation."

On that Sunday morning Mr Asquith had been reinforced by a letter from Bonar Law promising the Opposition's support in resisting German aggressive moves. This was morally helpful to the Prime Minister, since only a few days before Bonar Law had formally told Sir Edward Grey that he doubted whether the Tory rank and file would be unanimous in their support of war.

The dissidents in the Cabinet had been deeply impressed by the dramatic plight of Belgium, but the meeting still raged with doubts. Belgium's desperate insistence on avoiding entanglements had actually caused her to refuse to let General Jungbluth, head of her General Staff, attend the British manoeuvres two years earlier. No one knew whether Belgium would indeed resist an invasion, or merely capitulate under protest. The Belgian Government had made a curiously equivocal reply to the French offer of help, made the day before, saying: "We are sincerely grateful to the French Government for offering eventual support. In the actual circumstances, however, we do not propose to appeal to the guarantee of the Powers. The Belgian Government will decide later on the action they may think it necessary to take." While it was pitifully clear that this prim attitude was dictated by Belgium's desperate necessity not to provide Germany with the least excuse for alleging that she had departed from her formal neutrality, it provoked deep uncertainties among the British Ministers. Should Belgium decide, as was her perfect sovereign right, to choose the evil of submission as a lesser one than the evil of resistance, had Britain the right to impose on Belgium the miseries of a war for Britain's own purposes? It was fiercely argued that to force Belgium into resistance would be cruelly immoral, more particularly as there was no way in which Britain could provide her with immediate help.

So argued the doubting Ministers—Lord Morley, Lord Beauchamp, Sir John Simon, Mr Lloyd George, Mr Harcourt, Mr Herbert Samuel, Mr Pease, Mr McKinnon Wood and Mr Runciman.

All that Sunday the Germans were on the march. By half-past six that evening when the Cabinet met again it seemed virtually inescapable that the Germans would violate Belgian territory; almost as certain that the Belgians would resist. It could be, and was, still argued that the invasion might be "not substantial," that a simple traverse of a corner of Belgium might not constitute "intervention"—but it was casuistry and everyone knew it. It was impossible to envisage Belgium standing alone. Someone mentioned "gallant little Belgium"; the phrase endured for years, no one remembered the Congo. This was no longer a "Central European squabble."

On Sunday, 2nd August, the world's two most imposing and awesome Powers met head on at last. Germany declared war on Russia. Her armies moved over the frontier for the first time and violated Luxembourg, seizing the bridges on the Treves and Trois Vierges lines, and simultaneously announced that this was not considered to be a hostile act, but a simple protection of the railways. At the same time Russian patrols attacked the rail bridge over the Warthe near Eichenreid, on the Jarak-Wreschen line. Others fired on a German patrol near Prostken in East Prussia, three hundred yards on the German side.

Nothing could stop it now.

Yet Britain had to be convinced—her Parliament, her people; even her Cabinet.

That Sunday the Cabinet met twice. In the morning it was proposed at once that Sir Edward Grey be authorised to tell the by now distracted French Ambassador that we should in no circumstances permit any passage of German ships through the North Sea or the English Channel to attack the coasts or the shipping of France, and that the Navy be alerted to stand by for surprise attacks. All members of the Cabinet were in agreement but two: Lord Morley and Mr John Burns. Mr Burns immediately offered his resignation. He was induced to hold it back until the evening sitting. When Grey reported that he had in fact given M. Cambon that assurance, Mr Burns resigned. Lord Morley said he would sleep on his decision.

Mr Asquith was desperately anxious to maintain his Cabinet intact; almost hourly it grew more difficult. Its differences by now had crystallised into three parts: the small group that believed in military intervention if France was physically attacked, another that held that no circumstances whatever would justify such an action, and between them the main body of the Cabinet which held that Britain was under no obligation of any kind to intervene in a conflict between the European Alliances, and that her commitments to France were simply limited to guaranteeing her coastline against naval attack.

To this dilemma the Prime Minister had indeed contributed by his many public insistences that the European situation held no secrets: there were two great Alliances forever menacing each other, that Europe was bedevilled by a meaningless arms race, that the enduring threat was the growth of German naval strength, and that there was an Anglo-French entente, which should in no way be promoted into an alliance. He was to hear endlessly thereafter that a clear warning from Britain after the Austrian ultimatum to Serbia—that Britain would associate her armies with France and Russia—would have preserved peace. Always he maintained that Britain must remain uncommitted to the last moment, especially under a Liberal Government, in the diminishing hope of being able to act as mediator. It was nevertheless idle to deny that a tremendous issue of policy was involved, and that Sir Edward Grey shared with him the fear that with France destroyed and Germany controlling the Channel ports—with perhaps the French Navy added to her own—Britain would be in desperate danger.

But chiefly Asquith realised that a collapse of the Cabinet, necessarily involving his own resignation, would surely mean a war controlled by a Conservative administration— since the conditions were such that any kind of coalition was out of the question—and the country would be ruinously divided.

When the Cabinet met next morning most doubts had been resolved. Not all. John Burns had gone. Lord Morley announced, with regret, as he said, that he too must go as "We—that is I and the leading men in the Cabinet—do not mean the same thing in the foreign policy of the moment." Lord Beauchamp and Sir John Simon also resigned, though with less conviction. To fill the vacancies Mr Runciman was transferred to the Board of Trade; Lord Beauchamp succeeded Lord Morley as President of the Council. Two new members were introduced: Lord Emmott to the Office of Works, Lord Lucas to the Board of Agriculture.

That morning the King of the Belgians in Brussels telegraphed to King George in London:

> Mindful of the numerous marks of friendship of your Majesty and of your Majesty's predecessors, as well as the friendly attitude of Great Britain in 1870, and of the proofs of sympathy which she has once again shown us, I make the supreme appeal to the diplomatic intervention of your Majesty's Government to safeguard the neutrality of Belgium.

But this was 3rd August; if "diplomatic intervention" had ever been possible it was now too late. The Reichstag had met in the Weisser Saal of the Palace in Berlin to hear the speech from the Throne: "With heavy heart I have been compelled to mobilise my Army against a neighbour at whose side it has fought on many a battlefield. With genuine sorrow do I witness the end of a friendship which Germany loyally cherished. . . . We draw the sword with a clean conscience and clean hands."

Thus did Germany declare war on France.

6

Bank Holiday Monday had filled London with a sort of fantasy; the city was alive with restless people, gay and tormented, relaxed, tense, bewildered, thoughtful, carefree, obsessed; in the multitudes that moved back and forth along Whitehall was everything from enthusiasm to despair. The crowds accumulated from Trafalgar Square to St. Stephen's; by a sort of traditional gravitation they gathered outside Buckingham Palace, waiting for no one knew what sort of symbol. In Waterloo Station the two patterns of the day's life incongruously met and mingled: the holiday-makers in their boaters and brown boots, the children with their spades and pails, and the uncertain columns of sailors and Reservists carrying kitbags still stiff from the stores, their calves swathed in unfamiliar puttees.

There were others, involved at the same time less and more immediately. In the West End of London something like 2,000 Americans on business and holiday had been caught disastrously short by the ruinous complication of a simultaneous crisis and Bank Holiday, and were both rich and stranded. They plodded from hotel to hotel waving at-

78

tested cheque-books and valid letters of credit, but all cashiers were refusing paper that weekend. Finally they united in a desperate sort of mass meeting in the Waldorf Hotel, pleading poverty with their handbags full of diamonds, until the Consul was summoned to relieve them.

Outside the House of Commons the crowds grew thicker as the time grew near; what they were waiting for no one precisely knew. They jostled for the early evening editions; the lead stories said: "Britain stands in graver peril today than ever before." They flocked around the Members' entrance, cheering everyone, making way with loud cheerfulness as Winston Churchill arrived, arm in arm with F. E. Smith.

The Chamber inside was dressed for high drama. In the Gallery the Russian and French Ambassadors sat twelve feet apart, staring down. The House was densely packed from benches to floor. Questions were postponed; nothing mattered but the business of the day, the speech from the Foreign Secretary. They cheered politely as Grey walked in, reduced by fatigue to a ghostly grey. They cheered Mr Churchill, who sat flushed, twisting his Order Paper as he always did. They cheered the Prime Minister, carrying his white hair high, uncertain even then where his Government stood, and which of his Ministers would be with him three hours hence.

Swiftly the Moratorium Bill was hustled through all its stages, introduced by Lloyd George: the "Postponement of Payments Act, to suspend payments of Bills of Exchange and Payments in pursuit of other obligations." "The circumstances," said the Chancellor, "are well known to Members."

Sir Edward Grey rose, his eyes red-rimmed in a lined and empty face. He spoke for almost exactly an hour.

"We have consistently worked with a single mind to preserve peace. We have little difficulty in proving it, though little time was allowed . . . Austria showed a disposition to force things rapidly to an issue at great risk to peace. And the result is—the policy of peace has failed.

"I will not say where the blame seemed to lie," he said, "I will deal with British interests and honour." The Tory benches cheered. "I will deal with them free from passion." The Government benches cheered.

The week's negotiations would be published, he sighed. No secret engagement to support France would be sprung on the House. As far back as 1908, during the Bosnian crisis, Britain had told Russia that she could provide no more than diplomatic support.

"There was no promise," he said, "until yesterday."

France? "There is," he said, "our long-standing friendship with France," and there was a shout from the Labour bench: "And not with Germany?"

Grey's voice rose a trace in pitch. "Let every man look into his own heart. France is not the aggressor. Is a foreign fleet to be allowed to enter the English Channel? Are her north and west coasts to be bombarded—those coasts that are undefended because her fleets are keeping open the trade routes of the Mediterranean? Is that to be done under our eyes, with our arms folded?"

Grey paused for almost half a minute. "Yesterday," he said at last, "we let France know that we should not allow her coasts to be attacked. This is not a declaration of war. If Germany agrees not so to use her Fleet—should we give our pledge of neutrality?"

The Liberal and the Labour benches gave this a modified cheer: gave their approval to the last word. Then down came Grey's hand on the despatch box.

"It is far too narrow an engagement for us. If we run away, our respect is gone."

There was nothing left for Bonar Law to say.

"If it is to be war," he said flatly, "it will be forced upon us, and there will be no alternative."

Mr Redmond rose and very slowly said: "History is repeating itself. In the American War, Catholic and Protestant volunteers joined to help you. In our dire necessity, will you not withdraw your troops from Ireland? The Nationalists and the Ulster Volunteers will combine to defend her shores."

The lonely challenge came from the Labour leader. Ramsay MacDonald stood up very straight and said: "Your speech will echo in history, but you are wrong. Honour? No such crime is ever committed without an appeal to honour. It was so with the Crimean War, it was so with the South African War; it is so today."

At seven in the evening was the call of "Black Rod!"—the Lords had already passed the Moratorium Bill; the Commons moved out in procession, obeying the formula of tradition in the urgency of crisis. When they filed back Sir

Edward Grey announced: "Belgium refuses to accept a German violation on any terms"—but it was already in the evening papers; everybody knew.

There was just time for Mr Wedgwood to rise and cry: "There are seventy thousand people in the Potteries—my constituents. The poor will raid the country—for food!" And for Mr Edmund Harvey, the voice of Quakerism: "This is no people's war, sir. It is a war of men in high places, and bureaucrats."

It was described by Mr Balfour as "the dregs and lees of the debate."

That evening in Berlin thirty thousand Germans gathered round the Bismarck Monument to hear Dr Dohring, the Court Preacher, recite the Lord's Prayer, while far away the first of the Uhlans cantered into Flanders.

As soon as the House had risen Lord Beauchamp and Sir John Simon withdrew their resignations from the Cabinet.

At the Oval, Surrey was playing Kent in Jack Hobbs's benefit. The day ended with Surrey 472 for five, Hobbs b. Iremonger 226.

The next day the Oval was commandeered by the Army. The match was transferred to Lords.

As dusk fell, Sir Edward Grey, bent with exhaustion, stood at the window of his room in the Foreign Office with

J. A. Spender of the *Westminster Gazette*. He watched the warm summer's evening dissolve into London's evening dimness, and he said: "The lamps are going out all over Europe. We shall not see them lit again in our time."

That night Mr Asquith recorded in his faithful diary:

. . . we had an interesting Cabinet, as we got news that the Germans had entered Belgium and had announced that if necessary would push their way through by force of arms. This simplifies matters. We sent the Germans an ultimatum to expire at midnight requesting them to give a like assurance with the French that they would respect Belgian neutrality. They have invented a story that the French are meditating an invasion of Belgium and that they are acting only in self-defence, a manifest and transparent lie. Winston, who has got on all his war paint, is longing for a sea fight in the early hours of the morning to result in the sinking of the *Goeben*. The whole thing fills me with sadness. The House took the fresh news today very calmly and with a good deal of dignity, and we got through all business by half-past four.

An hour or two earlier Winston Churchill had replaced the Commander of the Home Fleet, Sir George Callaghan, by Sir John Jellicoe. For the moment, however, he was concerned about the Mediterranean. Somehow the French would have to put in line an army corps from North Africa, and their fleet must protect the movement. But both Churchill and the French well knew that in the Mediterranean was the *Goeben*, a German warship faster than anything the French possessed, which could break any transport operation. Already, on 2nd August, orders had gone out that everything must be done to shadow and intercept the *Goeben.*

Peace was ebbing away from a calm and starlit London. In the Prime Minister's room in the House of Commons Mr Asquith was sitting alone when his wife Margot entered.

She said, "So it's all up?"

He answered without looking up, "Yes, it's all up."

She sat down quietly beside him, and absently watched the backs of moving men through the half-open door. A secretary came in with the Foreign Office boxes, set them down without a word and went out of the room.

Asquith sat at his writing desk with a pen in his hand. As she watched him, his wife recorded, she wondered: what was he thinking of? His sons? Her son was too young to fight; would they all have to fight?

"I got up and leaned my head against his," she said, "and we could not speak for tears."

Late that night the Prime Minister went to the Cabinet room and waited with his wife and a few colleagues. Grey was with them, and Tyrrell, and Churchill, eager to flash his order to the Fleet.

At midnight Big Ben chimed out its long and hollow twelve over the restless city; England was at war.

In Berlin the British Ambassador paid a farewell visit to the Chancellor. He found him in deep agitation. "Just for a word Britain is going to make war on a kindred nation that asks only friendship. Just for a word: 'neutrality'! Just for a scrap of paper!"

It has been recorded that the morning of Tuesday, 4th August 1914, was one of the loveliest of the year; a warm sun in a cloudless sky and a temperate south-west wind, a modest temperature and a rising glass; the association of conditions that once in a while produces for England a brief moment of incomparable charm. By ten in the morning the crowds in Whitehall and the Mall were already vast; nothing like them had been since the night of Mafeking, though today they were not exultant but expectant, not rejoicing but uneasy, yet at the same time moved by the curious exhilaration that comes upon multitudes when some corporate drama imposes itself on the national scene. On that inexperienced August day there were yet no special forebodings, no legacy of cynicism to sour the fulness of the heart; patriotism was a simple and acceptable emotion, the easiest common factor of all. The crowds surged up the Mall to the space outside Buckingham Palace where, at ten forty-five exactly, the King in Council was signing the necessary documents that committed Great Britain to war.

By then the crowds were so huge and so demanding that the police were sent out among them to demand silence; nevertheless they continued to chant and cheer, and at eleven o'clock, which is for some reason the climactic moment of the English day, the King and Queen and the Prince of Wales appeared on the balcony. They waved briefly; the crowds applauded.

It was a curious moment; outside the Palace the citizens expressed themselves in a ritual enthusiasm; in the east of London other crowds, equally earnest but less uplifted, were besieging the food-shops. In spite of all the official reassurements the rush on the stores had begun in earnest, and trade inevitably reacted: butter was selling at two shillings a pound, eggs at two shillings a dozen; nearly half as much again as prices of the day before. On Monday sugar had been twopence halfpenny a pound; today it was sixpence halfpenny. The Home Office protested that supplies were ample, but already there were riots among shoppers in Hitchin and Bermondsey; a grocery in West Ham was sacked before noon.

Mr. Runciman, the new President of the Board of Trade, asked for, and immediately got, emergency powers to requisition all food supplies and to ration them should he deem it necessary, which at the time he did not. Food prices were fixed by law: sugar at fivepence a pound (within a week it was down to fourpence); butter at one-and-six-pence; cheese at ninepence halfpenny; lard at eightpence; margarine at tenpence; bacon at one-and-fourpence.

Asquith asked for, and equally swiftly got, a credit of £100,000,000 "for the general purposes of the war."

Lloyd George announced an issue of new "Bank Notes," in denominations of £1 and ten shillings, which became legal tender for the first time. When the banks reopened after the long Bank Holiday 3,000,000 of these were ready, and the presses were turning them out at the rate of 5,000,000 more a day. To begin with there was difficulty persuading the people that these certificates, or promissory notes (for that is all they were), represented honest money at all; they were regarded with great suspicion, especially in the countryside. True, they were legally convertible into gold, but the Chancellor heavily discouraged it.

The Bank Rate suddenly came down from 10% to 6%.

A Bill was unexpectedly introduced authorising the immediate spending of £4,000,000 to promote a housing scheme to mitigate unemployment. There was much talk of "the new Socialism"—and indeed before the country's eyes the foundations of the economy were shifting, the old fabric falling. The Government was now in business in hitherto unheard-of ways! It had taken over the insurance of ships at sea; it had taken over control of the railways; there was a moratorium on all debts except rent, rates, wages and taxes; much of the retail trade was under State control, and so were soon to be most sides of the citizen's normal life. The consummation that Grey had feared for the future, as he looked ahead beyond the war into the lowering shape of socialism, was already visible; the shadow of the thing, or the glow of its dawn, was already on the horizon of England, and the war was only two days old.

That day King George V received the Ambassador of the United States of America.

"My God, Mr Page," said the King, "what else could we *do?*"

The Prime Minister decided that the time had come to appoint a Minister of War. Since Seely had resigned after the Curragh troubles, Asquith had held the office himself, but it was clear now that he could no longer give it enough time, nor indeed enough ability. His first impulse was naturally to restore Haldane to the post, since the creation of the General Staff, the Territorials, indeed the whole organisation of the Army had been due to him, but the personal factors were overpowering—Haldane's preoccupation with German philosophy had already made him suspect; was he not a Hegelian? This was the age of superficial prejudice, of elementary emotional thinking; this was democracy. Haldane was held to be pro-German, as later Prince Louis of Battenberg was held to be pro-German. The public knew little of Haldane's worth and work (though both Haig and French did), and Haldane would not do.

Lord Kitchener was an appointment both expedient and wildly popular. He was a physically dramatic yet in some peculiar way personally unpretentious figure. He combined all the elements of British popular approval: a fierce and lowering appearance, a solid squareness of head and body, an established professionalism, a demeanour of inarticulate certainty, an impeccable record of domination and efficiency; an aloofness from the diplomatic scene. For above all Kitchener was not a politician. Implicitly that minatory expression and those uncompromising moustaches belonged to the field of action and not discussion; he was the more acceptable as a statesman because it was manifest he cared nothing for statesmanship. Kitchener, at that moment on leave from his post of Consul-General in Egypt, accepted the portfolio of War Minister without enthusiasm. He made it forcefully clear that he had no politics, and insisted that his place in Cairo be kept open for him. He had spent almost his whole adult life abroad—indeed he scarcely knew

England at all. He knew little of the recent War Office reforms nor indeed of Haldane, and it seemed he despised the Territorials. He called them the "Town Clerks' Army," and equated them with the elderly and decrepit French "territorials" who had impressed him so little in the past. As for the politicians: after one fruitless Cabinet dispute he is said to have announced that it "was repugnant to him to have to reveal military secrets to twenty-three gentlemen with whom he was barely acquainted."

However, of the qualities Kitchener lacked, none of them was foresight, or professional prophecy. From the very first he foresaw a long war—"It will take years," he told the Cabinet—and demanded a big army. He was, indeed, to oppose conscription; he was certainly to be astounded and appalled at the strange conception of trench warfare. When the time for that static nightmare came, he said to Sir Edward Grey, "I don't know what's to be done. This isn't *war*." Nor was it, by the standards of Kitchener of Khartoum, by the standards of the commander of India and South Africa, of the soldier whose brilliant professional triumphs had already provided him with civic grants from a grateful nation first of £30,000 and then again of £50,-000. This squalid business was not war as Kitchener knew it, even when he was drowned in the *Hampshire*, torpedoed on his way to Russia two years later.

"It is a hazardous experiment," wrote Asquith in his tireless diary, "but it is the best in the cricumstances."

To be sure, the dilemma was acute. The Army was restless; the scars of the Curragh incident had far from healed. There, the Army had won. When Asquith took over the War Office he could have reformed the whole Command, had not the international position been too tricky, the dangers of war too close. Curiously bad feelings existed. Lord Roberts would cut Sir John French in the street. Immense suspicion existed between the soldiers and the politicians, and the differences between the Staff and the Liberal Party was not an inconsiderable factor in those early days of war.

The old wars had been easier. Then it had been simple to differentiate the spheres of the military and the politicians; today it was almost impossible. Today meant citizen's armies, total war, the civilian *moral,* the industrial potential; a thousand imponderables.

Among them was the strange and tortured relationship between Field Marshal Sir John French, Britain's Commander-in-Chief, and Lieutenant-General Sir Douglas Haig, Commander of I Corps.

For nearly twenty years they had shared only one thing—a mutual dislike, and a mutual professional reluctance either to clarify or expose it. It was now fourteen years since French and Haig together had led the great ride to the relief of Kimberley; since the end of the South African War they had, by mutual decision, seen little of each other. Haig flinched from French's uncertain temper, distrusted his military knowledge, despised his personal character. Haig was fifty-three when the war began; he had learned many things in his Army career, but not the gift of self-expression in public. Instead, Haig did as many a school-girl or general had done before—kept silence and wrote in private. Haig may have been inarticulate, but he left diaries of three-quarters of a million words.

"In my heart," he wrote, "I know that French is quite unfit for this great command at a time of crisis in our nation's history."

As for Lieutenant-General Murray, Chief of the Imperial General Staff, Haig defined him as "an old woman," and told his diary so.

Questioned by the King, however, Haig merely grunted that "he had doubts" about Sir John French's appointment. Two days later he wrote: "However, I am determined to behave as I did in the South African War, namely, to be thoroughly loyal and do my duty as a subordinate should, trying all the time to see Sir John's good qualities and not his weak ones."

The War Council met at 10 Downing Street on Wednesday 5th August full of uncertainties and speculations. The legal situation was the only factor that seemed reasonably clear: war had actually been declared between England and Germany, between Russia and Germany, between France and Germany. Austria, however, whose initiative had precipitated everything, was as yet technically at war with no one at all except, of course, Serbia.

For years the "war of the future" theories had been based on a conventional hypothesis—40 per cent of Germany's strength would be used against France; 10 per cent of her forces and all the Austrian strength against Russia. Part of the French and Italian armies would be cancelled out keeping each other in check.

Up until a day or two before, all this had seemed rather

beside the point, since it had appeared that the centre of gravity was not to be on the Rhine or the Vistula but on the Lower Middle Danube. In the abstract war-game, fourteen Austrian army corps were to be arrayed in Galicia against Russia, which would allow Germany to leave only two of her army corps in the east and fling the rest of her force against the French. But this nice balance collapsed if Austria did not put those fourteen corps on the Galician frontier. Germany would have to make good the deficiency. Germany, everybody said, was in a very awkward position.

Up to four years before, Russia had comparatively neglected her southern theatre, assuming that war, when it came, would be primarily a Franco-Russo-German affair. Then she had changed her mind, withdrawn part of her forces to the heart of the country on the railways around Moscow, ready to be transported anywhere. The troops left in the Warsaw region were organised chiefly against Germany, pending action elsewhere. With the Austrian ultimatum that alternative seemed to have arisen. A Russian threat from Vinitza would cripple any Austrian advance on Serbia. The plains of Hungary were ideal for the extended Russian masses of horse. The last time Russian forces had been seen in Hungary they had been riding to the aid of Austria, to subdue a small nation that dreamed futilely of independence. . . . The war-game went on.

Now the invasion of Belgium had changed everything. The curtain had gone up, though no one knew it for certain, on the Schlieffen Plan—the Plan which was soon to become a legend, a conjurer's wand, a sort of military magic, invoking the invasion of Belgium as the keystone of German strategy and the infallible password to victory.

"Der Schlieffenplan," long in the archives of the German War Ministry, had been devised by Count Alfred Schlieffen during his office of Chief of Staff from 1891 to 1906; in later years when it came to be analysed in the light of its results it appeared less a certain recipe for success than a wild gamble, conceived wholly in military terms, and in contradiction to the theories of Schlieffen's predecessor, the elder von Moltke. Count Helmuth von Moltke had triumphed over Austria in 1866 and over France in 1870, by which time he had persuaded himself that this could not happen again, that Russia would not continue to stand aside while Germany disposed of her enemies in the West. Nevertheless von Moltke held that, since Germany's western front was defence against any French attack the bulk of his armies could be disposed against a Russian threat—it was a defensive policy, in accord with that of Bismarck after 1871.

From the moment Schlieffen took office he rejected this attitude, basing his theories on the firm dogma that no Power could possibly conduct a modern war for more than a week or two. It would be necessary, then, for Germany to accomplish a swift and complete victory against one enemy so that she might turn round with equal speed upon the other. And since Russia was too vast to be so overcome quickly, it would be necessary to project the entire German Army at once upon France. This reasoning was not necessarily dictated by the Franco-Russian alliance (which indeed did not exist when the plan was conceived); in any case Schlieffen was a military technician with no political interests whatever, except perhaps the usual Prussian contempt for the Austrian ally, who need scarcely be considered in a western war.

Schlieffen, banking on the sluggishness of Russian mobilisation, planned for seven-eighths of the German Army facing west; out of forty army corps only five would be left as a defence against Russia. The basic gamble was the destruction of the French armies at all cost—let the Austrians hold off the Czar's men in the east; let the Russians overrun all East Prussia, as far as the Vistula if they wanted. Let the French, indeed, overrun Alsace-Lorraine; even that would be of little moment when France was encircled, beleaguered and destroyed.

The elimination of France, however, presented difficulties. Her front on the Vosges was almost as impregnable as Germany's own—unless France were imprudent enough to take the offensive herself and submit to a defeat in the open field, and this France showed no inclination to do. To outflank France through the mountains of Switzerland was impossible, Schlieffen knew. He could turn the French front at Verdun by smashing through Luxembourg, but that would expose his own right flank, and furthermore if he could violate neutral Luxembourg the French could follow suit in Belgium. It would be therefore necessary to go through Belgium himself, or through Holland, along the Channel Coast. Far to the west of Paris ran the great encircling arrows of the Schlieffen Plan, finally sealing the city off, and all the armies therein.

The final draft of the Plan was finished by 1905, when indeed Russia had become almost negligible as a major Power. It still postulated an almost limitless reservoir of men, and what is more, as events ultimately proved, it was built on one extraordinary miscalculation, which was that the German troops could travel around the circumference of a great circle faster by roads than the French could cut across the radius by rail. There was to be much horror and catastrophe and heartbreak and fear before this fact emerged, as at last it did upon the Marne.

General-oberst von Moltke, nephew of the old Marshal, close friend of the Kaiser's Court, took over both Schlieffen's office and his plan, modifying it only by the elimination of the Holland invasion and, in the event, by compromising: 20 per cent fewer troops went west; 20 per cent more east.

In May von Moltke met the Austro-Hungarian Chief of Staff, Conrad. They had rarely met before. In their correspondence they had agreed that while war was probably inevitable it was not imminent; now von Moltke agreed that the time was near. Conrad asked how long his campaign against France would last, before he could join Austria against Russia. He was told: six weeks.

For those Radicals who were still arguing as war began that Britain could have preserved the neutrality of Belgium if she had not been obsessed by her commitments to France, von Moltke left a footnote to history, in a memorandum drafted in 1913:

> Should we renounce the march through Belgium, in case England promises neutrality? That would be very danger-ous, for it is uncertain whether England would keep her promise: but we should give up the only chance of a quick and decisive victory, which we need. Only if Eng-land went with us would a renunciation of the march through Belgium be possible. That, however, is incon-ceivable. . . .

But in August 1914 the French military intelligence had thoroughly miscalculated both the German intentions and the German strength. They proposed to mount their initial operations in Alsace-Lorraine, from their view the most propitious battleground.

The French, too, had their "Plan XVII"—a big east-ern offensive on either side of Metz by four armies, which was largely inspired by the old longing for the *revanche*, the recapture of the lost lands of Alsace-Lorraine, and also by the belief that the left flank could not be turned. The wrongness of that was even sooner to be proved.

Until the first shots were fired the British supposition had been that the French, being equal in numbers to the Germans, would hold up the advance fairly comfortably, while the British equally comfortably disposed of the Ger-man Fleet. Then, when the sea was secure and there seemed no remote danger of an invasion of England, the British Expeditionary Force could cross to France.

The war was only a matter of hours old when it became shockingly apparent that this leisurely approach was wholly impossible. The attack on Belgium had already upset all the plans; it was evident that Britain must reinforce the French at all speed. The Admiralty said guardedly that it could guarantee the crossing of the BEF, stipulating at first that two divisions must remain behind to repel any invasion of the country, but waiving this when the War Office argued that it must send all six divisions across as rapidly as possible. Though of course—it was pointed out —an operation of this nature would be seriously handicapped by Bank Holiday.

On the afternoon of the 6th, Asquith called all the Naval and Military high command, also Lord Roberts and Lord Kitchener, to Downing Street. He was informed it was safe to despatch at least four divisions under Field Marshal Sir John French. (Between then and the 20th all were moved; the fifth followed on the 20th; the sixth early in September.)

There was considerable argument as to where they should go. Kitchener wanted Amiens. Sir John French wanted the Maubeuge-Le Cateau area. General Joffre, appealed to urgently, took Sir John's view: the BEF should be concentrated at Maubeuge on the left of, and in touch with, the French 5th Army under General Lanrezac; by the fifteenth day of mobilisation it would move on towards the Meuse against the German right flank. General Headquarters would be set up at Vitry-le-François, in a schoolhouse by the pleasant banks of the Marne.

In the month of August 1914 the total ration strength

of the British Expeditionary Force was some 110,000. Rifle strength: 66,000; sabre strength: 7,600; guns: 400.

The Germans had 2,000,000 men on the move. They were only 700,000 conscripts; 1,300,000 reservists. The French, who had expected to have to deal with 60 divisions, found themselves opposed by 78 divisions, plus 14 *Landwehr* brigades. Against them General Joffre had 1,300,-000—of whom 700,000 were conscripts, 600,000 reservists. Another 1,200,000 reservists were called up, or waiting the call, but for them there was as yet no equipment, no arms, no officers. Worse, France's yearly increment from the new classes could be only 200,000 against the Germans' 500,000. There were, after all, only some 40,000,000 French citizens against a German population of 65,000,000. The Prussian generals in Bismarck's time alone had won three successful wars: against Denmark in 1864, against Austria in 1866, against France herself in 1870—all short, all victorious, all building up the German Empire into the mightiest Power on earth.

So the French Army moved in—the infantry still clad, and for a year to come, in *capotes*, heavy blue coats and scarlet trousers, like a Meissonier picture, trailing their *mousquetons;* artillery officers in gold and red, and invincible behind their revolutionary new gun, the .75; the cavalry gleaming still in steel cuirasses, horsetail plumes *en panache* from their Napoleonic helmets, their lances high—splendid to look at and magnificent, and outnumbered by three to two along the entire line of battle.

They had only to cast themselves directly on the foe,

it was said, and reduce him to helplessness with determination and the *Soixante-quinze*. Lorraine would be French again and victory would follow. The mood was such: Waterloo and Sedan might not have been; this was the spiritual reaction against the humiliations of the past.

But it came about that the French attack was to crumble to ruination while von Moltke's right wing curved behind them in the ordained sweep of the Schlieffen Plan.

In the five months of fighting in the year 1914 the Army of France lost 800,000 men, most of them in the Battle of the Frontiers.

France was not to recover from this for many a generation.

7

All over Britain, on walls and hoardings and the red backs of London General Omnibuses, there appeared a memorable poster: the brooding face of Lord Kitchener sombrely staring out above the fortifications of his moustaches with a demeanour somehow at the same time dedicated, challenging and reproachful. "Your King and Country Need You!" said the caption, below a pointing finger that for months to come was to follow Englishmen, patriotic or otherwise, wherever they might look. "In this crisis," it said, "your country calls on all unmarried men to rally round the Flag and enlist in the ranks of her Army."

There was no hint of compulsory service; Britain had never had nor approved of conscription, which was a system for servile Teutons or feckless Latins. Britain would always compensate for a small professional Army by the biggest Fleet in the world and by the judicious subsidising of Allies. It would, everyone knew in spite of Kitchener, be a short war. Indeed the most serious danger, for the inspired and keen young men, was that it might well be all over before they could get in.

100

The country seemed, for a while, to echo only to the sound of feet: the stamping feet of recruiting sergeants; the shuffling feet of volunteers, that somehow translated itself into the marching feet of recruits, drilling in temporary barracks, in the gardens of residential squares, drilling in the Temple, in ill-fitting uniforms and awkwardly-tied puttees, bound for adventure and excitement and boredom and misery and glory and ignominy and exaltation and fear and death for one shilling a day, and all found.

"Oh we don't want to lose you," sang Phyllis Dare, "but we think you ought to go . . ." There was a sudden vogue for white feathers.

The hierarchy of the Empire reacted with enthusiasm. The Indian Princes of Jodhpur, Bikaner, Patiala, Kishanghar and the Heir Apparent of Bhopal all volunteered; the Maharajah of Mysore offered fifty lakhs of rupees—£300,-000. Even the Dalai Lama of Tibet made a formal offer placing his prayers at the disposal of the Allies. The Kabaka of Buganda proposed to send all his tribe to fight; this was declined with cordial thanks. The New Zealand command caused great disappointment by refusing the enlistment of hundreds of huge Maori girls.

The BEF embarked at Newhaven, Dover, Southhampton, Bristol: the Army of a nation that had not fought a major war since Wellington's day. There were still hundreds of young officers desperate with impatience; fearful that they might not arrive in time, exasperated with a Government whose vacillation had made them already many days late; loudly worried lest the French should have disposed of the Germans before their chance should come. The BEF was small but it was the best-trained force in Europe, they said, ready to startle the world with its musketry, about to sail through the conscript armies of Germany as though on exercise. Why, had not the German gunners only recently started indirect fire? They could know nothing of such things; they still clung to mass formation; they never practiced extended order. You could not make a soldier in less than three years, and their infantry served for only two; what chance did they stand against the British seven-year men?

The ships slid up the Seine through the Norman country heavy with summer and came to Rouen in the morning mists—sirens blaring, bands playing, disembarking *abroad*, where the postmen waved and the toy trams clattered through the town and the women presented bouquets. The last time British soldiers had landed on the continent of Europe had been in the Crimean War sixty years before. It was ninety-nine years since a British force had landed in France—in 1815, after the defeat of Napoleon at Waterloo. It was the first time in France's military history that a French soldier could answer "Friend" to an English sentry.

The reporter of the *Echo de France* wrote: "Almost the entire public expected to see the big English fellows, dressed in red from head to foot, an excellent target for bullets. Instead, we saw strong, fresh and agile youths free from all haughtiness, and of a martial and resolute gait."

And the papers also said: "Huge victories in Alsace. Mulhouse captured. Twenty thousand German casualties." The French beamed; the young English officers said: *"Oui, c'est bien,"* with the lowering certainty that they had been right—the English were too late. They would be posted as pursuit troops at the best, or left behind with the *gardes-champêtres.*

Then they would be off through the night in a congested troop-train, jolting eastwards to Arras; past Arras to the railhead of the day; detraining and marching in fours on to this or that billeting village among the impassive peasants and the mobilisation posters: crossed tricolours, *"Armées de Terre et de Mer,"* and *"La Revanche!"* Not a villager was to be seen between eighteen and forty; all had gone to the war—somewhere. Marching all day over the eternal *pavé*, under the blazing cheerful sun, a third of the English were serving soldiers, tough and hard; the rest were reservists, their backs already fraying under the unaccustomed pack, buttocks galling at the steady rub, rub of the entrenching tool. The transport horses, still uneasy from the journey, fretted under the stiff new harness.

Almost imperceptibly, at first, came the new vibration to the ears, less a sound than a sensation, of infinite subtlety and suggestion: the gentle faraway grumble of the guns.

It travelled down those winding stumbling columns like an accolade, like a challenge, like a sentence of death; to every man there it was the moment of fulfilment or the hint of death. Ten thousand men sniffed the air and said, "Here is the war, and we are here." Far away over

the horizon the guns murmured and throbbed and oppressed the ear with a quiet irresistible persuasion; it was
far away, but it was still war.

As the first of the BEF was moving into Europe, the
British Ambassador to the Kaiser's court was moving out.
On 6th August Sir Edward Goschen took leave of Berlin.
The German Government put two saloons and a dining
car at his disposal, and a high official of the Foreign Office
came to see him off. It was a very civil leave-taking, though
the day before circumstances had been less urbane. After
Britain's declaration of war was announced, the Berlin
crowds had rushed up the Unter den Linden to the
Wilhelmstrasse and assaulted the British Embassy, calling
imprecations and smashing windows. They then moved on
and stoned the Hotel Adlon, for no especial reason, it
seemed, other than that the newspaper correspondents H.
W. Nevinson and Charles Tower were staying there. The
journalists were arrested, attacked by the crowd briefly,
and then escorted to the station to join the Ambassador's
train.

Before the train left for Holland the Kaiser's ADC
arrived with a message of qualified apology for the damage to the Embassy. It said:

> The Emperor wishes me to express to Your Excel-
> lency his regret for the occurrences of last night, but to
> tell you at the same time that you will gather from them
> an idea of the feelings of his people respecting the acts of
> Great Britain in joining with other nations against her old

Allies of Waterloo. His Majesty also begs that you will tell the King that he has been proud of the titles of British Field Marshal and British Admiral, but in consequence of what has occurred he must now divest himself of these titles.

(The Kaiser, however, had a sufficiency of uniforms and regalia left, since he was at that time an Emperor, a King, eighteen times a Duke, twice a Grand Duke, ten times a Count, fifteen times a Seigneur, and three times a Margrave.)

Then the war became an entrenched position among the stooks of corn behind a railway cutting, across the line of a county road, around the perimeter of a Flemish village, on the verges of a quiet canal. The trenches were hurriedly dug, badly dug; there was too much to watch and to stare at; so far too little to fear. Across the rolling open countryside lay the disputed lands of apprehension and doubt: across the skyline could be seen the cavalry patrols cantering from one position to another, and far away pillars of smoke rose calmly and vertically into the air from burning farms and steadings. Somebody said: that is the German fashion of signalling where their cavalry patrols have reached. And indeed the smoke seemed to rise in an enveloping curve: it might be so.

Far away above the horizon came a remote hint of drama—skyborne puffs of cotton-wool, appearing abruptly in the air full-borne, fading gently and almost reluctantly away: shell-bursts, shrapnel itself, without doubt, known so far only in theory, now visible in this pretty faraway form. One cut oneself a ledge in the back of the trench from which to study such a phenomenon in comfort— trenches had ledges; one had seen such devices in illustrations in the *Sphere* of the Balkan wars. Tomorrow one would improve it: recessing niches in the front parapet, against oblique fire—should such a thing arrive.

Far overhead a Taube aeroplane cruised insolently around, the black crosses visible on the wings—it was arrogant, it was useless; one shook one's fist and laughed: what could a flying-machine do? . . . The plane turned, in a slow circuit, and flew throbbing away towards the east.

Was this war, or what would war be? How did one picture the battle? Presumably one would lean solidly in one's trench, observing with a calm sardonic confidence the helpless approach of the German hordes, until the time came for the fifteen-rounds-rapid that was the culminating moment to which those endless musketry courses had led. Then would the land grow heavy with the corpses of the foe; one's own position encumbered with the piles of brass cartridge-cases; passed from man to man would be the rifles with barrels too hot to hold. Finally, and indomitably, one fixed one's bayonet. . . .

And then nothing whatever happened. The sun shone, the birds travelled busily through the sky; there in the high blue the delicate meaningless shell-bursts mingled imperceptibly with the drifting quiet clouds.

Until abruptly from the flank someone screamed,

"Down in the trenches!"—and in the same second a howl of horror overhead, and an unendurable explosion fifty yards in the rear, impossibly loud, outrageously perilous. This was the first spiritual knockout, the first terror, the first incredulous appreciation that those quiet and distant puffs of wool could be translated into this hideous roaring menace that sent a man grovelling and gasping to the dusty floor of his trench—spinning burning steel, tearing aside all illusion, opening up for the first time all the empty help-less vulnerable corners of the heart. Who ever knew that war made such a *noise?*

. . . And then of course it turned out to be one's own guns; a battery over the rise of which no one knew. The young officers rose unsteadily, sought amidst desperate in-security for the rational gesture, unstrapped field-glasses and stared over the parapet at the same empty rolling coun-try side, the same tranquil farmland fields. Someone had "cleared the foreground," thinned the hedges so that only the main stems should be left for an obstacle that yet gave no cover for an attack. And far away, past a belt of fir-trees, a sudden glimpse of horse—cavalry, in sections of fours, cantering away almost jauntily. Uhlans, one recognised the curious helmets; perhaps a squadron strength. The German Army, at last.

. . . Then there would be more guns, more furious sound, more terror; a short burst breaking and a sergeant suddenly bouncing and tumbling down the trench groping absurdly at the red mess where his face had been and dying with outraged inhuman protests as he rolled. Perhaps the

Taube had been watching, after all. And then nothing, for hour after hour after hour.

For the first fortnight of the Great War all the armies of Europe were gathering, arming, deploying, taking up stations. The momentum of war itself had not begun; only at Liége had it blazed savagely forth—and briefly, since the fortress of Liége was less impregnable than Joffre had believed, and the howitzer fire of the German siege artillery brought it down in seventy-two hours.

The papers went wild with overemphasis, overdramatisation, overenthusiasm; the German losses before Liége were reported as 25,000—by and by they were down to 5,000; nevertheless it was a "German rout."

Mr Asquith wrote to his wife in Scotland:

> I am disgusted with the optimism of the Press and other people, believing all this nonsense about Belgian victories and the Germans already demoralised or starving and committing suicide. All that has gone on so far, except at Liége, is mere affairs of outposts, and it looks today as if the Germans will be able to enter and occupy Brussels.

He therefore caused an official notice to be gazetted and publicised, saying:

> The public are warned against placing the slightest reliance on the many rumours that are current daily regarding alleged victories, or defeats, and the arrival of wounded men or of disabled ships in this country. They are, without exception, baseless. The public may be con-

fident that any news of successes overseas to the British Armies will be communicated officially without delay.

In the first week HMS *Amphion*, parent ship of the 3rd Torpedo Flotilla which had just sunk the German mine-layer *Königin Luise*, herself struck one of the *Luise*'s mines and went down in the North Sea with 130 lives. But a few days later the German submarine U-15 was rammed by the cruiser *Birmingham* north of Kinnaird's Head, Aberdeen-shire—the first U-boat loss of the war.

In London a warrant was issued for the embodiment of a force of Special Constables, and 30,000 men were sworn in within the Metropolitan Area, under Colonel Sir Edward Ward. They were each issued with one truncheon, one whistle, one notebook, one armlet and one warrant. All over Britain they suddenly appeared—bank managers, insurance agents, shop assistants, publicans, local squires and local poachers, mayors and dustmen, authors and painters and clerks and nurserymen and poets and solicitors, signing on after working hours to patrol the streets and the country lanes looking for what, so far, no one exactly knew.

While it was to some degree true that in August 1914 the German nation appeared to welcome war, as an extension of their national sense of confidence and pride in unity, that was not wholly so in Britain. Britain was in the war, but without the obligation of Alliances; no agreements existed either signed or verbal, and when it came to the point none had been necessary. (Nevertheless in the following month a formal agreement was signed with France and

Russia, at the instance of France, binding all three countries not to make a separate peace.) The war began without joy or exultation in London. Germany, doubtless, had bitten off more than she could chew. Thanks to Lord Haldane the BEF had 150,000 men. Nobody knew how short they were to be of guns and ammunition. Nobody, in those days, revealed that the Germans had something like 3,500 heavy pieces on the Western Front, infinitely more than the BEF. Armies, said the theorists, should have one heavy piece for each two light guns, with 1,000 rounds for each heavy and 2,000 for each light piece; the Staff knew there was not the slightest hope of achieving that equation before the summer of 1916. Even the *Official History of Military Operations* of that epoch defined the struggle as that "of a team of hastily-gathered amateurs who, guided only by a few professionals, had to learn by hard experience, against opponents who were a well-trained professional team."

Yet among the British population already could be observed a tremendous shift of opinion; the invasion of Belgium evoked a surge of emotion and outrage even among those who would in no way have been reconciled to a war of policy or interest. Even so, the mood of war did not overwhelm all questionings.

On 11th August George Bernard Shaw wrote to the *Daily News:*

> Our national trick of virtuous indignation is tiresome enough in peaceful party strife at home. At war it is ungallant and unpardonable. Let us take our pugnacity to

the field and leave our hypocrisy at home. This war is a Balance of Power war and nothing else.

The political influence of organised Labour at home must not be wasted in idle and exasperating platitudes about the wickedness of war, and the extravagance of big armaments, and the simplicity of non-intervention, and all the other splendid planks of the old Peace, Retrenchment and Reform platform. The wickedness of war is a reason for keeping out of war, but, the field once taken, it is not a practicable reason for betraying your Allies and your country by throwing down your arms and kneeling to pray.

Almost at once came the reply from his old contentious friend, H. G. Wells:

I find myself enthusiastic for this war against Prussian militarism. We are, I believe, assisting at the end of a vast, intolerable oppression upon civilisation. We are fighting to release Germany and all the world from the superstition that brutality and cynicism are the methods of success, that Imperialism is better than free citizenship, and conscripts better soldiers than free men. This war is not going to end in diplomacy, it is going to end diplomacy. At the end there will be no Conference of Europe on the old lines, but a Conference of the World.

This was high and elaborate talk for a nation on the edge of the most total and disastrous of recorded wars, at the same time horrified and unmoved, still manifestly incapable of adjusting its routine to an unprecedented situation—and, more surprisingly, apparently under no especial official pressure to do so. There were still tens of thousands of people in England to whom the outbreak of war was neither the long-awaited military orgasm nor yet an international political tragedy, to whom the whole business was a tiresome and indeed rather damaging aberration of which the chiefest manifestation was an interruption of business. The holiday resorts, for example, took considerable space in the newspapers to protest that "Everything was as usual." In spite of the headlines, desolate or strident, in spite of the speeches, the London, Brighton and South Coast Railway still advertised desperately: "Take Your Holidays As Usual"—and even then, and for many a month to come, while Europe writhed in its early misery, it remained simple and legal for a British civilian to book a ticket from Victoria to Boulogne and Paris. Or, indeed, from London to Australia: Nord-Deutscher-Lloyd's offered the passage from £17. This was not excessive, but then nothing was: on the Cornish Riviera Express the fare to Penzance was 28s.; a man could buy a suit to measure for 45s.; boots were 16s.9d. a pair, a shirt was anywhere between 3s.6d. and 8s.; dress fabrics were 1s.9d. a yard. If you smoked cigarettes, Players Navy Cut were threepence-halfpenny for ten (or Life-Ray at five for a penny); if you drove a car you could buy a two-seater Ford, now, for £125, or a five-seater for ten pounds more, and petrol was tenpence a gallon. A decent clerk could earn £2 a week easily, and so could an elementary schoolteacher, if he was lucky. He could rent a three-roomed house for ten shillings a week in a respectable district and for four shill-

ings in a slum, and landladies everywhere tumbled over themselves to lodge him for fifteen, all found. They were not
bad days, when 5,000,000 men in Europe were strapping
on their packs, and the early battles began to smoulder on
the Western Front.

On the 14th August, however, Field Marshal Sir John
French, as Commander-in-Chief of the British Expeditionary
Force, crossed over from Britain to France to establish his
battle headquarters at Maubeuge, as the "mobile left wing"
of the French Army. Next day he was followed by Lieutenant-General Sir Douglas Haig, Commander of I Corps,
who sailed on Napoleon's birthday to Le Havre.

Haig was obsessed by questions of theory: had the
British enough troops—even including the Belgians—to
wage a campaign independently of the French, or did the
British run the obvious risk of defeat in detail? What, for
example, did he know of the qualities of the Belgian Army,
except that it was nominally led by a gallant sovereign,
King Albert, and had a CIGS called Lieutenant-General
Chevalier de Selliers de Moranville: a resounding name,
never to be heard of again.

Haig cast a professional eye over the BEF; he saw what
neither Asquith nor Grey, nor for that matter Lloyd
George, could politically say: it was desperately short of
trained officers and NCOs, potentially short of both ammunition and guns; it was a splendid force that might yet
have to thrash around north-eastern Europe in a disastrously
gallant way. On the day Haig arrived the Saxon Jägers

attacked Dinant: it was a cavalry assault in the classic manner, with the German horse moving up behind hedges, avoiding the skylines. . . .

Sir John French called formally upon his battle-front neighbour, General Lanrezac, commander of the French fifth Army on his immediate right. It was perhaps one of the most disastrous social encounters of the entire war. Through a mutual opposition of characters, an unhappy apotheosis of national traits, through insensitivity or stupidity or inflexibility, perhaps through some simple and unhappy chemistry of personality, these two men formed an instantaneous and mutual dislike that was to colour their relationship for as long as it existed; it was inexplicable, painful, catastrophic.

So they met, the ruddy and forthright Englishman, the big and swarthy Frenchman, barren even of a common language. French spoke no French. Lanrezac spoke no English, had never been to England nor ever wanted to do so, admitted to an unshakeable prejudice against Englishmen of all kinds, considering them stubborn, arrogant and unreliable. It is the case that during the whole period of his command, Lanrezac never in fact saw one British unit. He was a sombre and obscure personality tinged from the start with a kind of resentful pessimism. Sir John French, himself a wholly conventional and unresilient soldier, felt under no obligation to concede the slightest trivial gesture to an awkward junior. Their meeting was a resounding failure, loaded with misunderstandings, productive only of a common determination to avoid one another at all costs. And indeed they did not meet again, side by side though their positions were, for more than a week, and then only because of a direct summons from Joffre.

This dismal encounter symbolised in some way the whole problem of Anglo-French co-operation, which in those early days seemed impossible. The different armies worked and operated on two wholly different technical levels; their ration scales were different, so were their logistics, their rates of pay, their systems of leave, their signals. The ranks mixed scarcely at all. They disliked and distrusted each other's food; the impenetrable differences between bread and wine on the one hand, and beef and tea on the other. The two armies even shared a common difficulty in identifying each other's uniforms, and had to be issued with printed postcards to avoid accidental encounters. In such circumstances co-operation could have been with difficulty accomplished even under tolerant and tactful high-ranking brothers-in-arms; under such mutually antipathetic commanders as French and Lanrezac it was, to begin with, almost impossible.

There was another bad omen for the British command: on 17th August the Commander of II Corps, Lieutenant-General Sir J. M. Grierson, without hearing a shot fired, died of an aneurism in the train between Rouen and Amiens. He was replaced by General Sir Horace Smith-Dorrien, who took over the following week at Bavai.

So the war began. The Belgians were falling back on Antwerp, the Germans were swarming over the Meuse around Huy and Liége, and moving on towards Brussels and Namur in a violent effort to turn the French left, which rested on Namur. What was happening, as the Germans squared up to the French wall, was just as had been debated for years by British military theorists, had been prophesied to the Cabinet by Kitchener, had been foreseen by Haig's lecturers at Camberley Staff College in the '90s. From Thionville, the Germans broke *right*, with a long right hook to sweep away Belgian resistance, an arm that was to grope down from Ghent to Amiens, aiming to the south-west of Paris, to embrace the French Army and drive it back to its own eastern borders, where the rest of Germany would crush and engulf it.

These were the considerations that pressed on Haig's brooding mind as he landed in Havre and reported to Tortoni's Hotel, and learned how alarmingly successful was the German advance.

The BEF began its move into Belgium on 21st August. For the troops it was exacting enough physically, simple militarily; fatiguing, but uneventful except for skirmishes with occasional Uhlan patrols.

Kitchener had issued a thoughtful and pious Order To Troops, to be kept at all times in the soldier's pay-book:

> Remember that the honour of the British Army depends on your conduct. . . . Keep on your guard against excesses. In this new experience you may find temptations both in wine and women. You must entirely resist both, and, while treating all women with perfect courtesy, you should avoid any intimacy.

When this Order fell into the hands of the French it caused great hilarity in the *popotes,* in those early days when there was still time and heart for laughter.

The BEF soldiered on, and as they tramped between the flat fields they chanted curious and improbable songs. Sometimes they were irreverent and frequently obscene, generally they were banal; they were many things but the one set of qualities that in no circumstances did they ever invoke was that of patriotism, honour or glory. The Germans might sing *"Die Wacht am Rhein";* the French and Belgians derived some fervent stimulation from *"La Marseillaise"* and the *"Brabançonne";* the BEF trudged along under that heavy summer sun to an inconsequential ditty called "Tipperary," a mild music-hall number the uproarious, passionate, almost immortal success of which was a mystery never in history to be explained, or indeed repeated. It had been written a year or two before by an obscure vaudeville composer called Jack Judge, and it had been sung by Miss Florrie Forde in the 1913 pantomime season at Douglas, Isle of Man, without causing any comment anywhere. True, it was easy to sing, it had no high nor low notes; its words reflected a mild but not too poignant nostalgia; above all it had nothing to do with battle. The fabulous triumph of "Tipperary" as the national anthem of Britain's first world war astonished Mr Judge to his dying day, and his publisher Mr Bert Feldman too. Very soon the sheet music of "Tipperary" was selling 10,000 copies a day.

By and by a serious-minded clergyman in London, deeming the melody proper but the sentiment inadequately pointed, produced an amended version:

> *Goodbye, self-indulgence;*
> *Farewell the soft armchair . . .*

To which the troops replied with the inevitable coda: "*Have a banana!*"

Up along the dusty roads between the poplars, behind the gun-limbers, towards the towns and villages ahead already torn and burning, towards the sacked and pillaged Louvain, towards the defence of honour and the barricades of human dignity, the BEF trudged, softly singing their anthem of liberty:

> "*Send for the boys of the Girls' Brigade*
> *To set old England free;*
> *Send for my mother, my sister or my brother*
> *But for God's sake don't send me.*"

The BEF moved up, and only the Staff were worried because the German Army was enfolding them, crawling around their left flank apparently unopposed.

The history of those opening days was one of misunderstandings, errors, disputes, irresolution, open quarrels, bafflement and heroism. The French Army was in fact, and not only in official legend, brave and steadfast. Yet Joffre—Papa Joffre, the calm and undismayed Commander —had drawn up his Plan XVII, entailing all manner of imprudent operations and offensives against forces vastly greater than his own, and by the time he had modified them, he had in a couple of weeks lost 300,000 men killed or captured. In the first month the French Army lost 10 per cent of its officer strength—1,041 killed, 2,679 wounded, 1,058 missing: 4,778 in all.

When the Germans began their attack on the eastern defences of Namur, the French believed that Brialmont's fortress would hold long enough for the fifth Army to cross the Sambre. They did not reckon on the huge shells the Central Powers could now employ, and which reduced Namur in three days' bombardment. General Ruffey's third Army ran into powerful German forces and was first halted, then driven back. The red *chenilles* on the HQ maps began to crawl faster west and south, and headed for the unblooded BEF. The BEF relied on Lanrezac to attack the flanks of the German columns crossing his front; Lanrezac showed a strange languor and the attack did not come. The French were now defending themselves desperately against attacks from the north and north-west.

The British had just approached the little Belgian township of Mons, capital of the province of Hainaut, when the Germans fell upon them.

On 23rd August Sir John French sent back the first signal of the retreat. Namur had fallen; he was in the gravest danger of being encircled; he feared for the safety of the Channel ports. He would pull back, he said, to a line Valenciennes-Longueville-Maubeuge. The picnic was over, and so soon. To almost all the soldiers of the BEF the war to which they were so newly come was, from the very start, retreat.

The withdrawal was orderly, despondent, uneasy. The men of the BEF knew nothing of the Schlieffen Plan, nor of Joffre's Plan XVII. They did not know that back in London Churchill and Kitchener had decided to land a brigade in Ostende, with the double purpose of encouraging the Belgians and harrying the Germans, who would think it a precursor of a massive force. They did not know that in fact 3,000 Marines had occupied Ostende, and that the armed liner *Kaiser Wilhelm* had been sunk by the *Highflyer* off the Belgian coast. They knew none of these things, but only that they were weary and disenchanted, men and horses oppressed by the endless heat, footsore and bewildered, sleepless and in retreat.

On 27th August a battalion of Munster Fusiliers, acting as a sort of rearguard, became detached from the main body of the 1st Guards Brigade. They fought for almost twelve continuous hours against huge odds, and died, as far as was ever learned, to a man.

The troops moved back along the road they had come, and with them, now, moved the people. As far along the road as could be seen, as far back as could be seen, the long columns of wagons crawled along, ground along through the hedgeless countryside. Across the fold of the fields an extended line of infantry was preparing a rearguard position, digging against time into the baked earth; and down the road beside the soldiers moved the endless train of vehicles, people, goods, fear, helplessness: *les réfugiés*. They emerged from the lanes, the service roads to the farms, the neighbourhood tracks; all the province was emptying itself onto the main stream, collapsing into flight. By and by two great currents were flowing back along the open road: on the right the twenty-mile column of military wagons, straight and well-horsed, bewildered but in order; on the left the vast random flood of retreat—vast farm-wains, loaded enormously with household goods, children, grandmothers dressed for despair in their black best; farm-drays drawn by oxen, by mules, by asses; pony-carts and dog-carts and hand-carts; decrepit landaus and victorias; bicycles and barrows—creaking axles, plodding feet, bent backs and burdens. For mile after mile the refugees clogged the roads, eyes down, remembering 1870. Behind them the mutter of gunfire grew to a rumble, then a growl; from time to time there was the coughing crash of the German howitzers, bringing a little death in a singularly dense cloud of sooty smoke. The French called them *marmites;* the British called them "Jack Johnsons."

When the military traffic grew double-banked, the refugees crushed off the road into the fields, staring mournfully, bitterly. Before every village door a cart stood being loaded. The old women followed the army wagons with angry hopeless eyes; they too could recognise a retreat.

That was the week of the BEF's miraculous escape. Mons could have been, almost was, a disaster; as it was the British lost 1,600 all ranks, and two guns. Sir John French sent a terse signal to General Lanrezac, whom he angrily held to have let him down, that if the British left flank was threatened more he would retire forthwith on his lines of communication, in which case it would be up to Lanrezac to look after his own left as best he could.

On 24th August a strange thing happened: a party of officials of the National Bank of Belgium in Antwerp appeared from nowhere, heavily burdened with money. They had followed the retreating armies to Namur, carrying 9,000,000 francs in cash for the governor. They arrived to find Namur surrendered and the governor vanished. Now they turned up at the French Fifth Army HQ in Le Cateau loaded with a great cargo of money and no idea of how to dispose of it. They would not hand it over to the Fifth Army paymaster. After a consultation they took armfuls of notes into the yard and, before the astonished eyes of the staff officers, burned it to ashes. They were still left, however, with 1,000,000 francs in gold, which resisted all efforts to burn it. Reluctantly they handed it over to the paymaster, and departed stiffly into the disintegrating countryside.

By now the retreat of the French Fifth Army was endangering the very existence of the BEF. Lieutenant E. L. Spears, the zealous liaison officer, was sent to see General Lanrezac personally and make the position clear; not an easy mission for a subaltern. At last, confronting the General in a schoolroom, Spears said: *"Mon Général,* if by your action the British Army is annihilated, England will never pardon France, and France will not be able to afford to pardon you."

Lanrezac, the withdrawn military theorist, had always

displayed a curious aversion to direct action; it seemed as though he could never bring himself to commit his arguments to positive test. Joffre, too, wearied of his negations, insisted on an end to delay. Lanrezac was compelled to order the attack, but it was already too late; the Germans had entered Valenciennes. The British began to fall back on Maubeuge. General von Kluck, of the German First Army, had ordered the capture of Maubeuge by the 24th. He failed. The exhausted British halted von Kluck's advance by twenty-four hours. They had neither food nor sleep in all that time, but they held up the Germans though six men in ten were Reservists.

The main body of the withdrawal remained controlled, but it was already disintegrating at the edges. Major General Allenby, GOC Cavalry Division, himself led the retreat as the head of the division, led by a French guide carrying a lantern. . . . Once a regiment of the BEF marched along a dusty road for several miles while on a parallel road another column marched at the same pace. So deep in dust were the uniforms that neither side recognised the other: one was British and the other German. . . .

Many groups of men, both French and British, found themselves cut off; by and by the countryside was sheltering many parties of what the French called *enfants perdus*, some alone, some in quite considerable numbers. Many surrendered, many died; many attempted to organise themselves into guerilla groups and to wage a furtive free-lance war against the German rear from hiding-places in the woods. A Captain Colbert, finding himself isolated early in the retreat, collected around him some 300 soldiers, mostly of the 205th Infantry Brigade: a strange raggle-taggle unit that remained more or less intact for over three months. The French command knew nothing of him until November, when somehow or other the Colbert group was heard of near Signyle-Petit, in the Ardennes. The 2eme Bureau believed it would be possible to get in touch with them, and an aeroplane was sent to deposit a volunteer, Sergeant Berthelot, of the 22nd Artillery Regiment. He landed in a forest clearing, met Colbert, and tried to organise a smash-and-grab raid on the German Supreme Command at Mézières. It failed, and the guerilla band broke up; most of them contrived to filter back one by one to the Dutch border, though Captain Colbert himself was captured and spent the rest of the war in a German camp. Sergeant Berthelot reached Amsterdam, contrived a passage to England and thence to Havre—where, naturally enough, he was promptly jailed as a spy. He argued his way out of that predicament, and was compensated at last with a Legion of Honour.

After this experiment many men were landed behind the lines. Crates of pigeons were parachuted, with instructions to any finder as to the kind of information that would be welcomed. To be found with a carrier-pigeon in any circumstances meant death to the peasants in German-occupied territory; nevertheless many of the pigeons found their way back to Intelligence HQ, and occasionally the information they bore was not spurious.

There was the extraordinary case of the British Trooper Fowler, of the 11th Hussars, who was cut off at Le Cateau, befriended by a villager called Madame Belmont-Gobert, to the serious danger of her life, and who remained hidden, semi-permanently concealed in a wardrobe two and a half feet broad and a foot and a half deep for nearly four years.

For the main body of the BEF every morning came the order: Hook in the transport and move west. Often the march lasted all the night. The British retreat was tougher than the French. They opposed more army, but they were better trained on manoeuvre and their musketry was good —so good that there were times when the Germans mistook rifle for machine-gun fire. The cavalry carried the same rifle as the infantry, and were trained to deploy on foot when necessary.

There was immense difficulty in supplying an army that had to use whatever roads it could. Soon the QMG hit on the plan of depositing dumps of provisions at likely passing-places, and the BEF tramped wearily past great sides of beef rotting in the fierce sun, dumps of bagged oats, corned beef, biscuit tins. The air was heavy with the smell of sweating horses—the great Clydesdales from brewers' drays and railway vans who had never learned to lean on their collars, who strained and gasped under the strange new military harness till the galls came and the flies ate them into holes, and thus they worked until they dropped. When they could go no farther, they were shot—this was the savage order of the Staff. The beasts must not fall into the enemy's hands, though in almost every farm on the road were draught horses that the BEF might not commandeer or even buy, to which the Germans would surely help themselves. The limping transport animals were led into the fields and destroyed. (When the German cavalry were retiring in their turn after the Marne, the British found their worn-out horses turned into the fields, grazing among the gunfire.)

The body was exhausted, and the spirit nearly so. Back to Maubeuge, to Pont-sur-Sambre, Le Cateau, back along the same familiar roads of the advance so small a time ago, with the chalk-marks of the brigade billeting officers still on the doors; back to Origny, Saint-Quentin, Coucy-le-Château—would it be back to Soissons on the line of the Aisne? Would it be back to the Pyrenees? That jest no longer sounded thin. Back to Meaux, deserted and dead— and with the local signposts saying: Paris—44 km., the distance of Reading to London. Château-Thierry—pillaged, looted, ravaged; furniture flung into the streets, a wild litter of empty bottles; an abandoned German helmet or two.

And at their feet, tranquil and serene and willow-hung, a little broader than the Thames at Henley, the river Marne.

It was during the first grim days of the retreat from Mons that, just a thousand miles away, the Russians began to press into East Prussia with two armies, under the Supreme Command of the Grand Duke Nicholas, uncle of the Czar. The German commander von Prittwitz lost control of the situation; he was replaced by Ludendorff, fresh from the conquest of Liége, and the old Hindenburg, called from retirement because he alone knew the dangerous terrain of the Masurian Lakes. They immediately decided to withdraw two army corps and a cavalry division from France. By the end of the month thirty-two trainloads of Germans were moving east.

Throughout the ranks of the BEF, and more so throughout the civilian population of Britain, a strange legend was born. The Russians were coming. The uncountable hordes of the Czarist armies were on the move to the defence of the west; indeed detachments of them had already set foot on British soil. From Scotland to the South Coast the phantom Russians were reported at second and third hand with extravagant corroborative detail—their bizarre fur hats had been seen on the quays of Leith, ghostly trains had passed through the Midlands, the windows crowded with bearded Slav faces, they had been detected trying to ram roubles into slot machines in London; their identity could not be doubted; some had even been seen, in that sultry baking August, with the snow still on their boots.

But in all Britain and France there was no Russian soldier; every one of the Czar's men was in East Prussia or Galicia, for the Battle of Tannenberg had begun, and the Russian Steamroller was grinding to its destruction. Almost every man was captured or killed, including General Samsonoff. The news did not pass the Allied censor; better the myth of the Cossacks with the snow-caked boots.

... 8

On that same day in France a Captain Helbronner, of General Lanrezac's staff, came to Sir Douglas Haig with a message: Lanrezac intended to give battle the next morning. Could he rely upon an effective British support? The captain found Haig just north of Ribemont near the village of Lucy, standing on a small mound, with an orderly holding his horses beside a lance planted in the ground flying his pennant, red with a white cross. A British airman was reporting that German columns had been observed advancing fast south west of Saint-Quentin.

Haig marked Helbronner's map, and said, "Go quickly to your general and give him this information. Let him take advantage of it right away. The enemy is exposing his flank as he advances. I am anxious to co-operate in his attack."

Haig nevertheless recognised that his infantry, fatigued from steady retreat, needed a few hours of rest, and sent a message to GHQ to that effect. He added that he could offer the support of his artillery and machine-guns if Sir John French, as Commander-in-Chief, approved.

The Commander-in-Chief replied, "No active operations of any arms except of a defensive nature will be undertaken tomorrow."

It was the first tangible opportunity of Allied co-operation in the field, and it went by default. Next day the French fought the battle of Guise, with no help from the BEF.

The next day came a peremptory message to Haig from the C.-in-C. "Please be good enough to inform the C.-in-C. how it is that any confidential promise of support by I Corps was made to General Lanrezac or why any official exchange of ideas was initiated without authority from Headquarters."

Haig replied curtly:

> I do not understand what you mean. I have initiated no exchange of ideas. GHQ not having secured from the French roads for the retirement of my Corps, I had for my own safety to enter into relations with the nearest French force on my right. As far as it was possible I have maintained touch with the left of these French troops—and due to the presence of this Corps their left has been protected ever since we left Maubeuge. My Corps still protects their left, and if the enemy advances from St. Quentin southward I shall have for my own safety to deploy guns etc. without asking for the authority of GHQ. The extrication of this Corps from the false position in which it is placed still demands the greatest exertion from us all, and my sole objective is to secure its retreat with honour to our arms. I therefore beg you will not give credit to such allegations as the one under reference without first ascertaining whether it is true or not.

It was one of the most stinging snubs ever delivered by a Corps commander to a Commander-in-Chief, and Sir John French had indeed to apologise personally the next day, after Haig had angrily driven thirty-five miles to see him at Compiègne.

The position had become critical both militarily and personally. Sir John French had achieved no sort of relationship with General Lanrezac and had greatly put up the back of Haig; furthermore he was now dangerously pressed by the advancing Germans. He was conscious of not being in Joffre's confidence, of not being able to see the whole picture. He was aware of the anomalous position of the BEF—a force autonomous, not subordinate, yet a unit in the French plan, dependent on French communications. He was obsessed by his dislike of Lanrezac, by his belief that he had been wantonly exposed. He was uneasily aware that the French for their part would accuse him of letting them down at a critical moment. In his mind's eye all the time was his order from the British Government: "The greatest care must be exercised towards a minimum of losses and wastage," since the BEF was the sole nucleus of any future British Army.

Finally, on 30th August, Sir John telegraphed back to London that he was about to withdraw his Army entirely from the fighting line and retire bodily behind the Seine.

He wrote to Kitchener:

> I cannot say that I am happy in the outlook as to the further prospects of the campaign in France. My confidence in the abilities of the leaders of the French Army

to carry this campaign to a successful conclusion is fast waning, and this is my real reason for the decision I have taken to move the British forces so far back. . . . Knowing what I do of the French soldiers' fighting capabilities and the immense amount of energy, skill, time and trouble which for many years has been brought to bear on their training and efficiency, I can attribute their constant failures to no other cause than defective higher leading.

The message brought consternation to the Cabinet. This would look like, and indeed would be, an abandonment of our Allies. Hastily Asquith conferred with Kitchener and Churchill, McKenna and Lloyd George. It was decided that the emergency was so great that Kitchener must himself go at once to French to see what could be saved from the mess. Kitchener went straight home from Downing Street, changed into uniform, and left from Charing Cross that night. He travelled by destroyer to Havre; he was in Paris by next noon, and was consulting with Sir John French in the British Embassy that afternoon.

By half-past seven that evening he was reporting to Asquith: "French's troops are now in the fighting line, where he will remain conforming to the movements of the French Army, though at the same time acting with caution to avoid being in any way unsupported by his flank."

Sir John French, however, was profoundly upset and chagrined, less by the countermanding of his decision than by the curiously simple fact that Lord Kitchener had arrived wearing Field Marshal's uniform. The Commander-in-Chief, outranked, went into a black and sombre sulk. It was a contingency that had not occurred to Kitchener, who had worn his uniform automatically, without considering the possibility that the functions of Field Marshal and War Minister might be confused. By and by Asquith was compelled to write a fulsome letter of conciliation to Sir John, saying:

> As Head of the Government I want you to know that you possess in the fullest measure our absolute and unreserved confidence, that we watch with ever-unceasing admiration your conduct of this arduous campaign, and we think the country fortunate in having at the head of the gallant forces a Commander who has never been surpassed in the capital qualities of initiative, tenacity, serenity, and resources.

This almost-Oriental lubrication restored Sir John's morale, a process completed shortly by the departure of General Lanrezac. The general's indecisiveness had finally exasperated Joffre himself, and quite abruptly he was *limogé*, the French equivalent of bowler-hatted, and replaced in the Fifth Army by General Franchet d'Espérey. This cheered Sir John greatly.

To England—though not for a while to France—came stimulating news: the first of the naval victories. The enterprise had been devised by Admiral Tyrwhitt, commanding the light cruisers and destroyers of the "Harwich Striking Force," and Commodore Keyes, head of the submarine service, who suggested to Churchill a "drive inshore to the enemy" in the Heligoland Bight.

Since the war began the British submarines had been probing the Bight; they knew that the Germans maintained there a flotilla of destroyers on all-night patrol, relieved each morning by another force. It was proposed that two flotillas of British destroyers and two light cruisers should put in near Sylt, deal with the outgoing German patrol, then turn west and destroy the incoming relief. Six British submarines were to take part, with the battleships *Invincible* and *New Zealand* from the Humber in support. Admiral Jellicoe offered three battle-cruisers and six light cruisers under Sir David Beatty.

At dawn on 28th August this enormous force sprang the surprise. The German battleships could not cross the bar because of low tide; they were trapped; only the light patrols in the Elbe and Ems could operate at all. The cruisers *Köln* and *Ariadne* were smashed by *Lion* and *Princess Royal*, the cruiser *Mainz* was sunk by the destroyers. Three more—*Frauenlob*, *Strassburg*, and *Stettin*—crawled home with many casualties. Not one British ship was seriously damaged. More than 1,000 German sailors died, including the Flotilla Admiral and Destroyer Commander. More than 200 were rescued and captured by Keyes in the destroyer *Lurcher*, among them the son of Admiral von Tirpitz, German Supreme Commander.

From this the German Fleet never fully recovered.

Not all the world was at war by any means. Much of it, in those early days, remained neutral, though its neutrality could be defined in four separate ways. Firstly there were those states not necessarily antagonistic to the Allies, but who were determined to stay outside the conflict, requiring no pressure to remain neutral; that is to say Spain and all the states of Central and South America, Holland (whose islands could have been of great military value), Norway and Denmark (who could have opened the Baltic to Britain, linked England with Russia, and made the blockade complete). Secondly were those states that were neutral at the time but whose sympathies were manifestly with Germany: Turkey, Bulgaria and Sweden. Thirdly, those states that were neutral at the outset but which had a tendency to associate themselves with Britain when the time became opportune: Greece, Italy, Rumania. Fourthly, and in a special category, was the United States, a nation so strong that its identity could not be affected by the course of the war, and whose final sympathy would in consequence be decisive.

Throughout the years of the war there were delicate and shifting relationships between Britain and the neutral states, and between the neutral states and each other, each relationship having different values for every month that passed. At the beginning the first difficulty was Holland; from the start Britain had had to assure the Dutch that she would not violate their neutrality so long as the Germans did not, though the temptation was considerable when the blockade became a factor in the war. At the same time Britain could not overtly support her neutrality as this would have compromised Holland in the eyes of the Germans and would indeed have been unwelcome.

In the second group each case was different, though the

major factor was of course Turkey. England, while not aware of Turkey's secret treaty with Germany, nevertheless feared the worst. It was clear that Enver Pasha, leader of the Young Turks since 1909, was eager to bring Turkey into the war at the side of Germany; long ago Grey had said that nothing short of Enver's death, presumably by assassination, could prevent this. Lord Kitchener laid immense stress on the importance of keeping Turkey neutral, at least until his Indian troops had been safely brought through the Suez Canal. Also it was highly desirable to avoid conflict with Islam and the Muslim world. From the start this was difficult, with the presence in Constantinople of the German warships *Goeben* and *Breslau*. For some months the diplomatic test was to delay Turkey's inevitable entry in the war, and at least to engineer circumstances so that it would, when the time came, be clear that Turkey's involvement came by her own aggression. In the event, this was manifestly from her own initiative—but by then the Indians were through the Canal.

The status of Egypt was curiously difficult. Her status vis-à-vis Turkey, in international law, had not been changed at all by the British occupation. After Turkey's entry into the war Egyptians became enemy subjects, but it would have been diplomatically unwise to have annexed Egypt physically, however simple an operation this would have been, because of the certain offence this would have caused in the Muslim world. Egypt, therefore, was declared a Protectorate; an ingenious compromise the by-products of which were to endure for another generation.

In the north-east of the Mediterranean everything was bedevilled by the inheritance of a generation of Balkan complications. Greece from the start made overtures to join the Allies, which was an embarrassing factor, in view of the delicate Turkish situation. In the middle of August her Prime Minister, M. Venizelos, offered all Greece's resources to the Entente powers, proposed a Balkan bloc of Greece, Rumania and Bulgaria—but even then the complications seemed insuperable, the rivalries mutually exclusive. Certainly Greece could dispose 250,000 men, and her ports would be valuable. It would of course precipitate the hostility of Turkey, but Turkey would declare her opposition sooner or later, anyhow. Nevertheless Sir Edward Grey said no. Every unit of this fragmentated neighbourhood was thinking only of *revanche* after the Balkan wars. Especially did Bulgaria demand concessions from Greece and Serbia, and this England could not in good heart guarantee; all England could offer was territory in Thrace then held by Turkey. And this was by no means what Bulgaria wanted; she was eager for an Aegean port and a slice of Macedonia, and this could be provided only at Greece's expense.

From the beginning Turkey was a somewhat shapeless factor in the forming pattern of allegiances. The Ottoman Empire was already moribund, its great empire of 100,000,000 souls effete and in disintegration, already dismembered by the Treaty of London, with the Balkan jackals nosing round its body.

The association between the German and Ottoman empires had been initiated by Wilhelm II and Abdul Hamid, but it was not seriously affected by Abdul's fall. After the Revolution, Enver Pasha went to Berlin and made many friends among the Pan-Germans, including the Crown Prince. In the first month of 1914 he became Minister of War, and was preparing to implement the agreement concluded three months earlier by his predecessor Izzet Pasha, whereby the German General Liman von Sanders would reorganise and command the Turkish forces, as the German General von der Goltz had done thirty years before. This arrangement brought angry protests from Russia, and a compromise was evolved. But Enver mobilised his army on the last day of July; two days later he had signed his secret alliance with Germany which was finally to commit him to intervention on the side of the Central Powers.

Enver, forever glancing over his shoulder at Russia, at the thousand-mile frontiers of land and sea between him and the ancient enemy, wanted above all things a victory over the Caucasus—and for that he must have control of the Black Sea, and for that he needed a Navy. His Navy was in England, in embryo. The two battleships that Britain was building for Turkey when war broke out were nearly ready. The *Reshadieh*, which Armstrongs were building on the Tyne, was in fact completed; the 500 Turkish crew were waiting there to take her over. For Winston Churchill in the Admiralty this was a difficult and challenging situation: the ships were technically the property of a neutral power, however certain Britain might be that they were potentially enemies. With a British margin over the Germans of only seven Dreadnoughts, Churchill decided that the risk was too great, and the Turkish ships were commandeered—legally enough, and under promise of compensation; nevertheless Turkey protested violently and was much chagrined, particularly as the ships had been paid for by a patriotic levy. King George, in some embarrassment, sent a personal message to the Sultan, regretting the necessity to seize his ships and promising that they should be restored after the war. (Still the Turks were not alone in this situation; at the same time British yards had three flotilla-leaders under order for Chile, four destroyers for Greece, three monitors for Brazil; the keels were also down for a Chilean battleship and a Dutch cruiser.)

Having immobilised all this potential force, Churchill turned his mind to the danger of the *Goeben* and the *Breslau*, now loose in the Mediterranean.

On 4th August the C.-in-C. signalled that *Indomitable* and *Indefatigable* were closely shadowing *Goeben* and *Breslau* at 37°44 N.—7°56 E.—that is to say somewhere between Algeria and Sardinia. He was told that war was imminent, that *Goeben* and *Breslau* were in no circumstances to be lost sight of, that they were almost certain to make attack on the French transports in the Mediterranean bringing troops from North Africa, and that at the first sign of such an attack the German ships were to be disposed of. Churchill felt confident enough, with sixteen twelve-inch guns ready for anything *Goeben* and *Breslau* might attempt.

But Admiral Souchon, the German Commander, made no such attempt, nor had he the slightest intention of so doing. He was off, at 24 knots, in the direction of Italy—

to the embarrassment of the British Fleet which, out of concern for Italian neutrality, could not approach within six miles of the Italian coast. By the morning of 5th August *Goeben* had reached Messina. Admiral Souchon had one immense advantage: he knew, which the British command did not, of the alliance now signed between Germany and Turkey. Souchon had one objective: to reach Constantinople as swiftly as might be.

At Messina he coaled from German colliers, taking thirty-six hours. The British light cruiser *Gloucester*, off the Straits of Messina, reported that the *Goeben* must be there. British battle-cruisers, under Sir Berkeley Milne, assembled off Pantelleria. In London Winston Churchill sent them fervent encouragement; the First Lord was under the impression that, since the British cruisers were helping the French fleet to protect French convoys, some form of liaison had been formed; in fact no French convoys had yet put to sea, and no British-French communication had been established. And when the *Goeben* and *Breslau* were trailed into Messina the British had still no orders to break Italian neutrality and follow them into the Straits.

On 6th August, then, Admiral Souchon steamed out of Messina with flags flying and bands playing, and with the British far away to the west. By next day's dawn he was on a fair course for the Dardanelles. Enver's problem was over. Over and over the Porte had heard the solemn warning: any intervention on the side of the Central Powers would mean the destruction and extinction of what remained of the Turkish Empire. Enver made his choice: three months later he was to set *Goeben* and *Breslau* against the Russian Black Sea ports and commit Turkey at last. The final paradox arrived at last: Russia and England together in the Black Sea; the old foes of Crimea uniting to drive the Turks forever over the Bosporus.

The Great War was a month old, and Paris was in acute danger. Paris, the greatest fortress in Europe, and indeed perhaps in the world, lay directly ahead of the advancing German Army—Paris which more than any other capital was the heart and physical centre of the nation, focus of all its communications. Her strong points made a great outer circle of 115 miles, a hard perimeter to encircle. There were three rings of defence: the city enclosure, then the group of 1870 forts, and beyond them the third line built in 1878, a succession of forty forts and batteries, masked batteries, trenches, abatis, and wire.

But the major forts were all to the east and north, from Villeneuve through Champigny to Montmorency and Ecouen. On the west there was practically nothing, and von Kluck was coming in from the west. Already his outrider patrols were almost within sight of the Eiffel Tower.

Paris was given the word from Poincaré: "Durer et tenir." But already the road to Tours was a river of refugees; for sixty unbroken miles the column of cars, carts, wagons, bicycles and plodding pedestrians inched to the south-west—following the example of the Government of France, which had already fled to Bordeaux.

General Galliéni, Military Governor of Paris, veteran conqueror of Madagascar, ordered the barbed-wire barricades to be put up at the gates of the city. There began a wild effort by the state printing presses to grind out maps of France; there were never enough, though thousands of accurate, far-sighted, useless maps of Germany lay stocked in the War Office vaults, prepared long ago for the offensive that had never come and now, it seemed, never would.

There was no immediate need to fear for foodstuffs. The Seine Department itself grew 14,000 acres of cereals, 7,000 acres of market garden, 1,600 acres of sugar beet. It had also 5,000 acres of meadow and 750 of vines. All this would last, if the outer ring held.

Paris itself began to congeal. The sight of the roadblocks on the outer fringe of the city brought the numbing realisation that the enemy was at the very gates; that the brave hopes of *la revanche* were gone. A million people had fled Paris, but another million remained, wondering when they would first see the helmets of the Uhlans. The streets were full of shuttered shops with written notices: *"Magasine fermé à cause de la mobilisation." "Tout personnel de la maison mobilisé." "Patron et trois fils au front des armées."*

The government of Paris was now at the Military Headquarters in the Invalides. Already it was doubtful of the ability of the city to endure what might well lie ahead, remembering the desperation and nervous collapses of the Commune. Stage by stage General Galliéni put Paris under

military law. The *terrasses* of all cafés were closed; bands
were forbidden in restaurants; all places of entertainment
had to close at eight at night; the sale of absinthe at any
hour was prohibited. Processions of any nature were
banned, "however patriotic their motive." There were
courts martial for "purveyors of false news"—whatever
that might be. There was no news, true or false; the censor
saw to that. The newspapers contended for a little while
with the wholesale blockage of information; by and by
they gave up, and three times a week Gustave Hervé
signed a column of blank paper, empty of text. No unpleas-
ant truths might be told, no defeats acknowledged. The
great hotels–the Majestic, the Astoria, Claridges, the Conti-
nental—were converted into hospitals, splendidly equipped,
lavishly overstaffed with skilled surgeons and society
infirmières, but the weeks passed and no wounded came.
The casualties poured into Orléans and Tours by the
thousand every day, but the Paris hospitals remained empty;
Paris must not be demoralised, and the hospital trains were
diverted all over the country so that Paris should not be
made neurotic by the spectacle of the wreck of war.

Ordinary life grated slower and slower; as more men
were called up more factories closed in La Villette and
Charenton. The Government promised an allowance of one
franc twenty-five centimes to women dependent on soldiers
—a shilling a day, and even that was hard to come by, waiting in line outside the *mairies* for the forms, the stamps.
For other women things grew harder yet, for dancers,

singers, prostitutes; there was no social life, no men; there were not even any Germans.

On the last day of August a German aeroplane flew insolently low over Paris and dropped a notice: the German Army, it said, would arrive in three days.

General Galliéni, faced with the great emergency, was yet a sanguine and resourceful man. It seemed to him that the Germans, having not enough men to surround Paris and not enough heavy artillery pieces to reduce it, would logically attempt to destroy the defending armies, and to do this von Kluck must pass between Paris and the great fortress of Verdun. As he did so, he must present his right flank square on to Paris, and this Galliéni seized on as his only chance.

He sent an urgent message to Joffre at Supreme HQ at Bar-sur-Aube. And he prepared to move his own garrison not inwards, but out.

Galliéni had men, but no transport; the army's trucks and wagons were floundering down miles away in the departments of the Oise and the Aisne. In Paris, however, that first September day, there were 2,000 taxi-cabs.

Many were never to take another fare. Some were to return, long after, to the boulevards. That day every taxi in Paris vanished from circulation, was commandeered by Galliéni and sent to war.

Into each cab were packed five soldiers; four inside and one beside the driver, with rifles and kit, *capotes* and rations. The bizarre fleet moved out in convoys, like growling and coughing chariots, north-east through the Porte de Pantin, out into the countryside where no taxi had been before.

Ten thousand soldiers were moved that day to Meaux, on the banks of the river Marne.

One more strange development was to occur before the Battle of the Marne and the turn of the tide: there came the news that a party of Germans were approaching the French Fifth Army HQ at Orbais under a flag of truce, and by and by two German cars drove up with a white pennant, with two officers and a sergeant blindfolded, according to the usages of war. The officers were Captain von Arnim and Captain von Kümmer; the sergeant was a one-time comic singer by the name of Slewing from the Berlin music-halls. They were all three highly nervous.

They were taken to the château headquarters where Lanrezac was waiting for them; the bandages were removed, salutes were exchanged. The Germans said that their mission was to request the immediate surrender of Rheims, that it might be spared destruction by shelling.

Lanrezac dismissed them. He did not say that he had no intention anyway of defending Rheims, that indeed it had already been evacuated.

The French corps commander conducting the German truce party through the lines abruptly decided that their documents were not in order, that they had been observing French positions, and held them as spies. As a reprisal General von Plettenberg, waiting outside Rheims, began to shell the undefended city, unaware that the French had gone, that General von Hausen's Saxon troops were already in occupation. The infuriated Saxons, believing themselves under fire from the French, seized the mayor. A head-quarters order into Rheims demanded the instant return of the truce party—of which neither the mayor nor the Saxons had ever heard—under pain of execution of the mayor and ten hostages. The Kaiser's headquarters announced in addition that if harm befell the truce party, 300 French officer prisoners would be shot.

At that point Joffre intervened. He established that the German party had in fact behaved irregularly; they were finally repatriated through Bordeaux by a neutral ship. The city of Rheims was fined by the Germans the sum of 50,000,000 francs.

That was the end of Lanrezac, the vague, baffled man whose brief command saw only defeat and despair.

On 4th September General Franchet d'Espérey took over the Fifth Army in its bleakest hour. He at once sent a message to Sir John French in most cordial tones, which greatly heartened Sir John, already cheered by the news of Lanrezac's departure. Sir John had been low, immensely discouraged; the long retreat had taken the heart from him. He knew that the French Government had left for Bordeaux. He realised that by so obviously avoiding Paris, von Kluck intended to destroy the French armies or drive them into Switzerland. He suspected that Joffre was about to declare Paris an open city; he feared that he had possibly ordered the abandonment of Verdun. Sir John French's heart was full of the deepest misgivings.

Immediately on his appointment General d'Espérey called personally on Sir John at his headquarters in Bray-sur-Seine. He was a fierce and confident man, in every way different from the indecisive Lanrezac; furthermore for the visit he had taken the trouble to wear his K.C.V.O.

The tide had surely turned for Sir John French. On that 4th September Marshal Joffre put out his Order of the Day Number 6, ordering that battle at last be joined, that the Allied armies turn about and face the enemy. The following day he too left Supreme HQ at Châtillon-sur-Seine and drove to see Sir John.

They all met standing in a chairless room in Sir John's Château Vaux-le-Peuil in Bray—Joffre, French, the British CIGS General Murray, Major-General Wilson, and Joffre's Chief of Staff, General Gamelin.

In his flat low voice Joffre set out his *aperçu*. The First German Army under von Kluck had abandoned the approach on Paris and had veered to the south-east, groping for the French left flank. D'Espérey's Fifth Army was now north of the Seine, preparing for a frontal attack on the Germans. To its left the British were collected between the Marne and the Seine, themselves flanked on the left by the taxi-cab army from Paris. The strategic situation, said Joffre with care, could be worse. The Germans' lines of communication were stretched, the French communications were good. What he did not say was that he was oppressed by doubts about the performance of the British Army, and about the manifest despondency of its Commander-in-Chief.

Joffre said he had come to thank Sir John French for

his readiness to co-operate in an action on which might depend the fate of Europe. Now the Allied forces, from Paris to Verdun, would turn about at last. Corps and regiments would move forthwith into position. The time for retreat was over. Tomorrow, at six A.M., the new war would begin. Those who could not advance were to stand fast, and die if necessary *en place*. There would not be another metre of withdrawal.

At the end of it the old Marshal—he was sixty-two—turned his tired eyes on Sir John and said abruptly: "*Monsieur le Maréchal, c'est la France qui vous supplie.*"

Sir John, quite overcome, turned on the interpreter and exclaimed: "Damn it, I can't explain. Tell him that all men can do our fellows will do."

They shook hands.

"But tell him," said Sir John, "that my forces can't be ready by six; we'll have to make it nine."

The Battle of the Marne was defined by Winston Churchill as the greatest battle that was ever fought in the history of the world. The forces engaged in it exceeded anything that had ever been seen before. The impulse was desperation; the risks involved were incalculable. The day before it began Joffre telegraphed to the Ministry of War in Paris: "The struggle which is about to take place may have decisive results. It may also, in the case of a reverse, have the gravest consequences for the country."

The battle began on 5th September, as the summer faded gently over the fields from which no harvest had been taken, over a front of 200 miles, with one end in Paris and the other in Verdun. Forty-nine Allied divisions and eight cavalry divisions faced forty-eight German divisions and seven cavalry divisions. The French and British soldiers, dispirited and weary from the long retreat, were one day stumbling westwards to defeat, the next facing east against a German force that was in the full confidence of triumph.

Early on the 5th General Maunoury's Sixth Army went into action on the Ourcq.

The British were to advance in three echelons, preceded by cavalry, in the direction of Montmirail. As soon as the Sixth Army had its footing on the Ourcq, the British were to move on Rebais, while d'Espérey took his Fifth in on frontal attack to Montmirail, with Foch on his right. The general order went out: all impedimenta was to be sent back; the units were to advance with only ammunition, supplies for a day, and ambulances to follow the troops. All civilian conveyances encountered were to be pitilessly thrown from the road. Defaulters were to be summarily shot. Heroes were to be summarily rewarded on the field. No circumstances would justify retreat. The attack began.

By the evening of the 5th the German command became aware that something in the situation had changed, the momentum had diminished, the French were no longer being herded towards Switzerland, the British were no longer plodding in retreat. Von Kluck and von Bülow, heading south with the First and Second armies, were ordered to swing round and face Paris. Von Kluck, unexpectedly brushing a French force that should not have been within miles, found his flank guard astonishingly reeling back seven miles, with considerable loss.

General-oberst von Moltke, back in the Emperor's Supreme Headquarters in Luxembourg, was startled. The German army had two corps, 80,000 men, immobilised in Antwerp, for even von Moltke could not wholly ignore the wild stories of projected Russian landings on the Belgian coast. Two more corps had been withdrawn from the West to face the Russians in East Prussia; they did not in fact arrive until after Tannenberg, so they might as well have stayed where they were. Von Moltke still persisted in his assault against General Castelnau's Second French Army in Lorraine; four more days were to pass before he detached two more corps and hurried them west.

The attack from the Paris direction on von Kluck grew fiercer; he suddenly realised his protection was going and pulled back two corps across the Marne to form to the north. Von Bülow, next in line, found himself with his right flank in the air. A gap began to form between von Kluck's left and von Bülow's right; it increased as men were moved to meet Maunoury's attack; soon it was thirty miles wide, manned only by cavalry and a few infantry divisions.

Far away on the extreme left of the German line was Prince Rupprecht with his Bavarians of the German Sixth Army; north-east of Verdun the Crown Prince Wilhelm was held down.

Into the gap between the two main armies of the German right advanced the BEF, with some of d'Espérey's Fifth Army. Five British divisions were preceded by five brigades of cavalry. One hundred and twenty thousand men moved up in fifteen-mile columns, and the German cavalry and the Jägers were driven back, for the first time in the war.

Suddenly the weather broke, and the flat farmlands softened into mud, with the ditches lined with dead. Hundreds of British soldiers, having lost their greatcoats or abandoned them through the heat of the summer retreat, were forced to protect themselves with sacks, or rummage through deserted houses for old clothes, forcing their way into empty farmhouses where the abandoned dogs remained still chained to the doors, savage with hunger. Advance, they learned, was a bloodier thing than retreat, demanding more in endurance and resolution and resistance to terror, coarsening and degrading those whom the constant presence of dirty death did not ennoble through their wretchedness, filling the brief pauses of exhaustion with questions. Why am I here? And how can I continue? The answer had to be found in discipline, in training, but tactical training could go so far only; always it had to ignore the greatest factor of all: fear. Why does a bullet kill? What is the difference between Christ crucified and a dead infantryman hanging from the wire? Wounds, too, were rarely as the battle-paintings had shown, the sabre-cut on the brow, but complex and brutal and unutterably foul. The BEF advanced towards the Aisne through a new world; by and by it seemed that they had lived there since time began.

And who was the enemy, the man ahead? The French

could hate, and with reason, but in the BEF to begin with there was as yet no special formula for hate, no personal animus against "Jerry" (for that is what he was; only officers and the Government called him "Hun"). "Jerry" symbolised the impossible ambivalence of the British soldier, endowing the enemy with a mad kind of affectionate tolerance—Jerry was an odd bloke, but he was possibly no worse than the French and Belgian allies, often doubtless better. Jerry took the heroics from that early war, where still the company commander led his men into action with drawn sword. Jerry, too, was the nameless private, the Poor Bloody Infantryman, blundering through the stinking mud that was one day to bury him.

By 7th September the British had entered Coulommiers. It was pillaged, and so littered with empty bottles that it became known, for a day or two, as the Champ des Bouteilles. The next day Montmirail fell to the French. The advance accelerated over a countryside still unmarked by trenches, the trampled cornfields still relatively unpocked with shell craters, where the unburied dead lay green and grotesque on the open fields, awaiting the burial units of the *gardes-champêtres*.

In four days the British advanced forty miles, and lost 2,000 men, which was fewer than French or Haig had believed possible.

At no time did it appear to occur to the Allied command that a thirty-mile gap between two strong armies would form a perilous salient for the attackers, vulnerable to fearsome cross-fire, that it could be a trap. The extraordinary thing is that it did not appear to occur to the Germans either.

On 9th September General d'Espérey proclaimed:

> On the historic fields of Montmirail and Vauchamps, which a century ago witnessed the victory of our fathers over the Prussians of Blücher, your offensive has broken the enemy's resistance. Held on his wings, his centre broken, he is flying to the east and north by forced marches . . .

Nevertheless Foch, on Maunoury's right, was in heavy difficulties, pressed dangerously by the Duke of Württemberg's Fourth Army. At one time he was nearly compelled to give way under vicious bayonet charges. "My flanks are turned," said Foch, "my centre gives way; my position is desperate—I attack."

The Germans had begun their big retreat; the famous divisions from Hanover and Westphalia and Brandenburg were hastening back to the Aisne, and the Allies were in pursuit.

Rheims now lay ahead for the taking. The French insisted on a triumphal entry, with General d'Espérey at the head of his cavalry, but the anticlimax was terrible—there were no crowds, no applause, no garlands; the inhabitants of Rheims were numb with privation and fear. Too many hostages had already suffered. Hundreds of citizens still sheltered in the enormous cellars of the champagne houses, and hundreds more, who did not, were killed in the markets when the German shells began to crash into the town. The bombardment fell on the cathedral. The French ordered that the 1,500 German prisoners be moved from the town hall cellars into the cathedral, hoping thus to protect it; the shells continued to fall. Soon HQ had to move from Rheims to the village of Romigny.

Every day was a new spy-scare. Dozens of citizens were arrested on suspicion; if there was not instant and overwhelming proof of innocence, they were shot. No one invoked justice; there was no time; the nation's existence was at stake, and if only one in twenty suspects was guilty, that was one danger the less. When the BEF caught suspects, they were handed over to the French.

The Battle of the Marne was over; the pursuit faded away on the banks of the Aisne. There the Germans halted, rallied. Back in Luxembourg General von Moltke, shattered by the collapse of his *blitzkrieg*, fell ill in spirit and body and was replaced as Chief of Staff by the Minister of War, Falkenhayn.

In Washington the German Ambassador, Count Bernstorff, sounded the United States Government for an intervention on the basis of the *status quo*—and the French Ambassador, M. Jusserand, replied bitterly that France would accept a return to the *status quo* when Germany could undertake to restore life to the French dead.

Slowly the battle crystallised along the Aisne. There, on the farther bank, awaited four long years of stalemate, of immobility, of trench warfare, of wretchedness and indecisive death.

By the beginning of September, London, at least, had recovered from its first numbness. After only four weeks,
the war seemed already part of the fantastic new background to life, at once outrageous and incomprehensible,
stimulating and horrifying, for the early blows were absorbed and the worst horrors yet to come. The lights reap-
peared in Leicester Square and Piccadilly, for DORA—the
Defence of the Realm Act, that was to set a seemingly
permanent repressive pattern for British social life—was
still feeling her way; there were fewer cars and taxi-cabs
to be seen, but not inconveniently so, and the presence of
so many men in uniform at every music-hall gave a kind of
justification to those who were not. Nevertheless a curious
uncertainty informed every official exhortation: the people
were urged to remain calm, but not too calm—that could
suggest apathy. They must not agitate themselves, yet must
be forever up and doing. They should renounce organised
sport, yet they must play games for fitness' sake. They
must practice economy, for money spent was money
wasted; at the same time they must not too harshly cut their

154

expenditure, as that would precipitate industrial distress. They must be cheerful yet serious, concerned yet tranquil. They must no longer think of their own affairs, while strenuously maintaining business as usual.

In any case most people were insulated from the more lowering truths. Facts were contraband; the censorship took care of that. Mr F. E. Smith was the first Director of the Press Bureau. In September he was succeeded by the Solicitor General, Sir Stanley Buckmaster. Both of them based their operations on the system of the smokescreen and their announcements on the theory of the euphemism: the enemy would suffer "defeats" but the Allies sustained "reverses"; the enemy would "retreat," the Allies would "retire." When the baffled and helpless BEF was being forced backward every day on the dreary road from Mons to Montmirail there were released in London tales of "doggedness," and few enough of them. When September saw them in pusuit of von Kluck and von Bülow, the censorship opened its doors again to anecdotes of heroism. Both were true indeed; nevertheless the newspapers protested daily, as newspapers have always done, with varying motives, that the British people were capable of standing the truth. No one, however, knew just what that was; hardly the papers, perhaps not even the censor; certainly not the tired and bewildered soldier trudging now towards the Aisne, content if at least he knew where Company HQ was to be found.

The London theatre swiftly accommodated itself to the patriotic mood. By September the Lyceum was running *Tommy Atkins*, and Seymour Hicks had produced

England Expects. The music-hall created a wholly new London archetype: the K-nut—tall and languid in morning coat and grey tophat, last in line of the Dandies, Bucks, Swells, Bloods and Mashers. He was presented by Basil Hallam at the Palace in *The Passing Show,* singing, "I'm Gilbert, the Filbert, the Nut with a K—The pride of Piccadilly, the blasé roué . . ." For a while every young man was a Knut, until the war reached out and took him, and absorbed him, and overwhelmed him—as it did Basil Hallam himself, the first Fop, crashing ultimately to his death in an observation balloon shot down on the Western Front, and a generation of Gilbert the Filberts died with him in the mud of Passchendaele.

In the meantime, however, the great moment of music-hall came twice nightly: there would fall a backcloth of a Union Jack, and before it would stride an actor in the uniform of a naval officer, strangely carrying a bat. "Cricket for the time must end. *This* is the wicket we must defend!" It was banal, but the applause was not. This at least was something the Germans could hardly imitate.

In September the recruiting figures had reached 30,000 men a day. By halfway through the month Britain had sent to France 213,000 men and 57,000 horses. Already, by the end of the Marne, 17,000 men were casualties.

In Oxford more than London, perhaps, could be seen the dead hand of war. With hundreds of the existing undergraduates gone, now drilling with wooden rifles in the parks of provincial townships, the colleges seemed oddly empty; this year the University had 1,800 fewer students than ever before, and one or two new men found themselves plodding alone up empty staircases and across desolate quads. There was no University football, no prospect whatever of the Torpids or the College Eights; the Boat Race itself had been cancelled. Here and there a few convalescent wounded sat in the grounds of New College, watching the fumbling manoeuvres of the recruits in Kitchener's Army.

What news there was from France was grim, revealing strange new aspects of human behaviour. The Germans in their advance through Belgium and France had provided enough material for horror: the sack of Louvain, the destruction of Rheims, the violation of a hundred villages and townships; and the press did not stint itself in stories of violence, mayhem, rapine and plunder. Much of it was true, much was coloured almost beyond credibility. The time came when some observers, shocked as they were with the facts, were driven to protest.

H. N. Brailsford, most respected of reporters, wrote:

> . . . I might be persuaded to believe that some German officers might violate women when carousing in safety after a victory, but to assert that an officer can have leisure first to violate and then mutilate a girl, under fire, in the heat of battle, three hundred yards from the enemy lines, is to assert what is obviously impossible. The burning of Louvain and Aarschot are indubitable facts. I invite the reader to recollect that under pressure of a supposed military necessity we ourselves burned every farmhouse and some small towns in the Transvaal and the Free State. These severities will remain a hideous stain on German renown. But they prove not so much the peculiar and ex-

ceptional savagery of the Germans as the brutality of all war. . . .

Unexpectedly, the German Staff became sensitive enough to the allegations of atrocious behaviour to commission a small group of the neutral American observers who had flocked into Europe to enquire into their accuracy. Their conclusions, which they later published, were that many of the allegations, of the nature which the history of wars everywhere and at all times had made familiar, were fundamentally true, in the sense that newly-occupied towns and villages were generally treated roughly. The soldiers would come in mad with thirst; when the beer was consumed they would drink whatever came to hand, and there seemed little check on their drunkenness, and consequent pillage and rape. Charges of deliberate torture were rarely substantiated. It was established that it was not unusual for troops to march into occupation of a village behind a screen of captured women and children, to discourage snipers and francs-tireurs. It was concluded that much premeditated brutality was undertaken as an act of policy for the purpose of intimidating the civilian population; it had frequently been effective, and the Belgian Army had been considerably hampered in its operations by the wild appeals of non-combatants that the fighting should take place in any neighbourhood but their own.

Twenty-two German universities drew up a protest against the accusations and distributed it to all foreign universities: "You will be convinced with us that where the German troops have had to accomplish work of destruction they acted according to the pitiless laws of defense in war."

Yet still each occupied village saw its hostages arrested, its proclamations offering the threat of death.

To the British soldier in general the mass behaviour of the Germans presented all manner of paradoxes. As an individual he excited no especial emotion of any kind. Apart from the fact that his hourly objective was to kill one, there seemed nothing particularly outrageous about him—and then the BEF would retake a township and be confronted with confusion far more than the impersonal destruction of high explosive, with all evidence of random looting and rapine and defilement, and it could only be concluded that the German soldier was impelled by some driving necessity always to act as he felt the part demanded. From time to time he would consider himself the mediaeval *Landsträger*, living hard and drinking deep and going mad; but equally probably at the next encounter he would be a Teuton knight or a spellbound Lutheran. The BEF was not deceived by the horrifying word-pictures distributed in Britain by the Press Bureau, and even more furiously in the French papers. Jerry was a coarse bastard, but if he was the undisciplined sot he was said to be, would he make such a superbly professional job of his sandbag barricades and his trenching, would he stand in his defensive positions so resolutely and long?

At home there were many considerations more immediate. England, still far from the noise and blood and dirt of war, compensated for its immunity by sudden wild

and widespread scares. There would be attack from the air
—for weeks Southern England went about its business
staring at the sky. That such a thing had never happened
did not mean that it never could. The Admiralty had to
issue a notice: "A British naval Air Ship will make short
cruises over London in the next days by day and by night,
but there is no necessity for public alarm, and on no account should it be fired upon."

No such reassurance, however, could arrest the sudden
tremendous epidemic of spy fever that swept England
during the early autumn of that year. England—an island,
yet a cosmopolitan centre, a political sandbank on which
all the dubious elements of Europe could logically silt up—
abruptly England felt herself the centre of espionage activities, and with a certain reason, since spies there were in
abundance. For a turbulent month, however, spies were
anyone who looked unorthodox, who spoke with a thick
intonation, who was, had been, or could have been German.
In the first week of war there were round-ups in Dover,
Penarth, Falmouth, Portsmouth, Barrow, Sheerness, Swan-
sea, Cardiff, London; there was a considerable haul of
waiters and barbers and such like. Many of them had lived
in Britain for thirty years without taking out their papers;
now they learned the penalty of their oversight. It became
dismally necessary for the Carlton and Ritz Hotels to publish an announcement saying: "There is not a single person
of German or Austrian birth, whether naturalised or not,
employed in our establishments." The Board of the Hotel
Cecil swiftly followed up by announcing that "it had felt it

necessary to dispense with the services of German and
Austrian employees." These exalted examples set the tone
for every pull-up and tea-room in England, which fell
over themselves to dismiss anyone remotely suspect of alien
blood, not a hard thing to detect in the catering trade. It
in no way prevented the most violent riots in Brixton and
Deptford and the Old Kent Road, where thousands of
patriots loyally destroyed every suspect butcher's and
delicatessen shop in sight. Tremendous damage was done,
until contingents of police and Army Service Corps were
sent in to tranquillize the areas.

Finally the Home Office had to publish a curiously
diffident and convoluted *dementi:*

> The secrecy which it has hitherto been desirable to
> observe [it said] cannot any longer be maintained, owing
> to the evidence which it is necessary to produce in cases
> against spies that are now pending . . .
>
> It was clearly ascertained five years ago [said this of-
> ficial statement] that the Germans were making great
> efforts to establish a system of espionage in this country.
> In order to trace and thwart these efforts a Special Intel-
> ligence Department was established by the Admiralty and
> the War Office . . .

What was defined by the tortuous expressions that
followed was that in 1911 the passing of the Official Secrets
Act, up to then confused and defective, was rationalised so
to embrace every possible heard-of or unheard-of method
of moving information to the enemy. In those three years
from 1911 to 1914—said this solemn handout—the ramifica-

tions of the elaborate German espionage network in England had been discovered, and agents had been watched and supervised long before the outbreak of war. There were something like a couple of hundred of them known to the police; of them twenty known spies were arrested, some two hundred interned. The Government explained its curious dilemma: it was difficult to bring anyone to trial because the ensuing evidence as to their detection would have hampered the Intelligence in their work. They were merely held as prisoners under the Aliens' Restriction Act. As some said, it was far too good for them.

The Aliens' Restriction Act empowered the Home Office and police to prevent all aliens leaving or entering the country; should they be already there, they must possess neither wireless-telegraphy apparatus nor carrier-pigeons.

Espionage was by statute made a military offence, triable by court martial, with penalties varying from life imprisonment to death. The public was formally requested that anyone with suspicions should communicate them to the local police. A Government order was issued: every alien bearing an Anglicised name assumed since the war must surrender it, and resume the name by which he had been known before the war. Reluctantly, yet immediately, a hundred Heinrichs who had become Henrys abandoned the euphemism; dozens of Godfreys reverted to Gottfried; many a Scott had, only the other day, been a Scholy. About 1,200 Germans, Austrians and Hungarians—good and bad, sympathetic and treacherous, honest or subtle, but by and large innocent and unaware—were arrested, taken to

Olympia first, distributed around the camps. All over London confused and baffled hairdressers, waiters, porters, sausage-manufacturers, either trembled in their shoes or gave themselves up. They saw that Karl Gustave Ernst, barber in the Caledonian Road and one of the first men arrested, had gone down for seven years, while the wilder press bayed its applause. They also had the terrifying example of Ernst Kludas, a middle-aged tradesman who had spent all his adult life in Ramsgate, who hanged himself in his downstairs cupboard, so that his wife might retrieve her British nationality. That was not unusual; it was reported frequently enough. Hugo Krebs and his wife Alice were fined £25 each in Hastings for failing to comply with the Aliens' Restriction Order; Krebs paid the fines, returned home and cut his throat. He had explained to his wife that he could think of nothing else to do.

"Another matter which has engaged the closest attention of the police," said the official statement, "has been the possibility of conspiracies to effect Outrage. Yet no trace whatever"—said the report, in its own italics—"has been discovered of any such conspiracy and no outrage of any sort has been committed by any alien—not even telegraph wires. . . ."

Nevertheless by the end of the war's first month 9,000 Germans and Austrians of military age had been arrested and taken into detention camps, mostly in the Isle of Man.

Some produced a rather fearful kind of drama. There was Carl Hans Lody, publicly tried by court martial before Lord Ceylesmore and nine officers, in circumstances that revealed to thousands of startled Englishmen the impulses that can drive a man equally patriotic and reckless. Carl Lody was accused of attempting to convey information calculated to be useful to the enemy from various parts of Britain and Ireland; the absorbing factor of his trial was the gradual revelation of how abysmally stupid even a spy can be. He wrote almost all of his painfully incriminating letters *en clair*, he posted them to palpably suspect addresses in Stockholm or Helsingfors; he kept his personal luggage undisguisedly full of annotated newspapers and compromising notebooks. When he was finally—almost reluctantly—arrested, and when he was court-martialled, nothing much could be said for his subtlety but that in these cruelly obvious letters he had, at least, signed himself with a code name. The code name meant nothing at the time, being merely an affectionate corruption of the name of his German lover, Natalie. But in years to come it was to seem as though somewhere a sinister star had skipped in its course, for Carl Lody, the German spy of the year 1914, had unsuspectingly signed his name Nazi.

He had no defence, except that his counsel, asking for less than the supreme sentence, said that Lody was a German, and had only too clearly deceived no one. He said no word at all in his own defence, but sometimes stood upright and bravely, and sometimes wavered in fatigue. No verdict was made public; a week later it was announced that he had been executed by firing-squad in the Tower. He was only the first.

An anti-German emotion, then, both mad and comprehensible, spread through the country; it crushed little Islington hairdressers and Soho waiters and Chelsea cinema-theatre owners, and finally it turned, as was perhaps inevitable, on the highest available vulnerable target: the person of the First Sea Lord of the Admiralty.

Prince Louis of Battenberg was German; that is to say, in his veins the blood ran 100 per cent that was somewhat diluted in the British Royal Family, of whom he was—as indeed at the time it seemed who was not—a kinsman. The selection of Prince Louis for popular abuse was perhaps a strange rationalisation of many things; in a state ruled by a family whose intricate and abundant genealogical pattern was punctuated throughout by Schleswig-Glucksburgs, Saxe-Meiningens, Oldenburgs, Brunswicks, Hesses, Schaumburg-Lippes, and Schleswig-Holstein-Sönderborg-Augustenburgs, that the one individual among this convoluted network of collaterals who was effectively working in the nation's cause and intrinsically part of the organic establishment should become the target of a violent campaign of denigration, suspicion and odium, and should have been so speedily destroyed.

Prince Louis had been born in Graz sixty years before, son of Prince Alexander of Hesse; he had become a naturalised British subject at the age of fourteen, and had joined the Navy as soon as possible, where he greatly prospered in spite of, as was sometimes said, having to learn his English as he went along. He served in the Egyptian War of 1882;

he was Naval Adviser to the Inspector-General of Fortifications in 1893; Director of Naval Intelligence in 1902; Rear-
Admiral in 1904. In 1907 he was Second-in-Command of
the Mediterranean Station; the following year he was flying
his flag as C.-in-C. Atlantic Fleet. In 1911 Churchill offered
him the job of Second Sea Lord and the following year,
when Admiral Sir Francis Bridgeman retired through illness,
Prince Louis succeeded him.

He was, however, clearly Germanic, if not German,
and the thing was anomalous—or at any rate perverse to
those patriots who readily ignored the interlocking factors
of relationship in European royalty so long as they kept
their heads down and did not intrude on the war. Indeed,
their argument was logical enough: Prince Louis had married his cousin Princess Victoria—and although she was the
granddaughter of Queen Victoria she was nevertheless
sister to Prince Henry of Prussia, the Kaiser's brother, and
he was High Admiral of the German Navy. It could be
argued that if the service hierarchy of the conflicting European Powers was to be overlapped by the royal hierarchy
then these exasperating paradoxes were almost inevitable.
Only the cynics did so argue, however; to the rest, Britain's
fleet was being run by a Hun. It was said loudly in the press,
less loudly in the clubs.

The Navy itself was well enough content, or at least its
younger and more progressive element. Prince Louis was a
technician. He was interested in Naval aviation—he was in
fact the first Flag Officer to fly. Even before the climax his

friends were by inference defending him. There had been an occasion during a courtesy visit to Germany when a German Admiral had reproached Louis for being in the Royal Navy at all, to which he was said to have replied, "Sir, when I joined the Royal Navy in 1868 the German Empire did not exist."

The end of that last July had presented the First Lord with perhaps his grimmest professional dilemma. The normal procedure was for the ships at the end of their manoeuvres to disperse to home ports for leave, reducing their complements to maintenance parties only. On July 25th, two days before this was due, Prince Louis decided to remain at the Admiralty. Churchill had gone to Cromer, where his wife was unwell, leaving his service colleague in charge. The Austrian ultimatum was due to expire that Saturday at six in the evening. Louis waited in his office, racked by the decision: should he maintain the Fleet in a condition of mobilisation? If he did, it might be provocative enough to produce the spark; if he did not there would be left in England a Fleet dispersed and helpless.

When Churchill telephoned from Cromer at lunchtime, Louis recommended that the Fleet be kept in readiness. Churchill agreed, saying that he would return by evening. The signal went out to the C.-in-C. Home Fleet in Portland: no ship would leave anchorage until further notice. By the early hours of 3rd August the mobilisation of the Navy on a war footing was complete.

The anti-German campaign that was to burn through

the country then took some time to reach the feet of the First Sea Lord, but elsewhere it was not slow in starting. Before the war was five days old the War Office sent its formal proposal to the King that his cousin the Kaiser and all his family be deprived of all honorary rank in the British Army—and, by inference, vice versa. Prince Louis was an honorary Hessian Colonel. He had been forty-six years in the Royal Navy. Nevertheless, if German pastrycooks were to be persecuted, this fact must be remembered.

The War Office proposal seemed undeniably reasonable; nevertheless the King chose this almost superficial issue on which to be oddly obdurate. The German royal names, he said, should remain on the army list until they resigned. Lord Roberts, by this time qualified as a grand old man and past all personal interest, was sent to ask the King to reconsider his decision. Finally the King agreed to drop the enemy names from the next edition of the army list, so long as there should be no proclamation. The whole matter was in the context of the time so trivial and protoculaire that it might have escaped notice had not a public outcry been stimulated about the presence in St George's Chapel at Windsor of the Garter Banners of the enemy Princes. The King still insisted that, as symbols of history, the banners should remain above the stalls, whereupon the *Daily Mail* and *John Bull*, as watchdogs of the public conscience, suggested a patriotic raid upon the chapel. It was in fact not until May 1915 that the King, under urgent pressure from the Prime Minister, consented to a notice that the names of the eight enemy knights be struck from the roll of the Order and their banners removed. He still insisted that their name-plates and titles remain on the stalls.

None of this had passed Prince Louis by; the First Sea Lord remained vulnerable. Soon there came the early reverses at sea. Three cruisers were torpedoed in the North Sea; Admiral Cradock's little fleet was lost at Coronel. The wilder press returned to its work: Prince Louis was accused of incompetence if not worse. Could it not be treachery? How, it was demanded, could Britain trust its Navy to a Sea Lord who was brother-in-law to the man who ran the German Navy? The *Globe* decided to make an open attack on Louis, on the very day on which it carried the news of the death of his nephew. Prince Maurice, son of Louis's brother Prince Henry, died of wounds received in the Mons retreat. "Distinguished Member of Royal Family," the *Globe* said, "Dies in Action."

After some two months of high-level whispering and low-level vociferation, abetted by a steady flow of anony-mous letters, Prince Louis wrote to the First Lord:

October 28th 1914

Dear Mr. Churchill:

I have lately been driven to the painful conclusion that at this juncture my birth and parentage have the ef-fect of impairing in some respects my usefulness to the Board of Admiralty. In these circumstances I feel it to be my duty, as a loyal subject of His Majesty, to resign the office of First Sea Lord, hoping thereby to facilitate the task of the administration of the great Service to which I have dedicated my life, and to ease the burden of H. M. Ministers.

It was a succinct and indeed dignified signal, and Mr. Churchill, responsive to a genuinely dramatic gesture honestly and artistically realised, replied:

October 29th 1914

My dear Prince Louis:

This is no ordinary war, but a struggle between nations for life or death. It raises passions between races of the most dreadful kind. It effaces the old landmarks and frontiers of our civilisation.

I cannot further oppose the wish you have during the last few weeks expressed to me to be released from the burden of responsibility which you have borne thus far with so much honour and success. The anxieties and toils which rest upon the Naval administration of our country are in themselves enough to try a man's spirit, and when to them are added the ineradicable difficulties of which you speak, I could not at this juncture in fairness ask you to support them.

The Navy of today, and still more the Navy of tomorrow, bears the imprint of your touch. The enormous impending influx of capital ships, the score of 30-knot cruisers, the destroyers and submarines unequalled in modern construction which are coming now to hand are the result of labours which we have had in common, and in which the Board of Admiralty owe so much to your aid.

The first step which secured the timely concentration of the Fleet was taken by you.

I must express publicly my deep indebtedness to you, and the pain I feel at the severance of our three years' official association. In all the circumstances you are right in your decision. The spirit in which you have acted is the same in which Prince Maurice of Battenberg has given his life to our cause, and in which your gallant son is now serving with the Fleet. [His son, Prince George, was serving in the *New Zealand*.]

I beg you to accept my profound respect, and that of our colleagues on the Board.

Thus did the First Lord, with what can only be described as a reluctant alacrity, take leave of his embarrassingly Teutonic colleague. Prince Louis was at once replaced by Lord Fisher, in spite of the protests of the King, who did not like Fisher. The press, assuaged, turned to other matters.

On that day the entry in King George's diary read:

Spent a most worrying and trying day. . . . At 11.30 saw Winston Churchill who informed me that Louis of Battenberg had resigned his appointment as First Sea Lord. The Press and Public have so many things against his being born a German, and that he ought not to be at the head of the Navy, that it was best for him to go. I feel deeply for him; there is no more loyal man in the country. . . . At 4.30 I saw poor Louis, very painful interview. I told him I would make him a Privy Councillor to show the confidence I had in him, which pleased him. . . .

That was effectively the last ever heard of Prince Louis of Battenberg. From then on he made neither complaint nor comment. There was, to be sure, a letter to the *Times* protesting at what the writer called "an injustice"—from a Labour politician called J. H. Thomas, whom Louis had never met.

Prince Louis and his wife retired at once to Kent House,

on the Osborne estate on the Isle of Wight, which had descended to her from Queen Victoria's mother. There the lady occupied herself with Red Cross work and the unobtrusive production of a history of Naval medals. There was, after all, an Admiral of the Fleet's retirement pay of £2,000 a year.

Later—in the following year, when the same pressures were borne along on an even more strongly illogical emotion, so that the King himself had to change his name from Wettin to Windsor—all the royal relatives with German cognomens surrendered them for a peerage, including the late First Sea Lord. The titles of Serene Highness and Prince were traded in for that of the Marquess of Milford Haven. Battenberg, by the simplest switching, became Mountbatten; thus did Prince Louis's younger son become Lord Louis Mountbatten, by which he was to be remembered even after the achievement of his own viscountcy thirty years later.

... 10

When the German High Command appreciated that its chance to envelop and destroy the Allied armies had gone, it abruptly changed its primary plan, switched the direction and axis of its attack and amended its objective. Its desperate preoccupation now was to turn the Allied left, secure the coast, prepare a new road to the heart of France. The Germans had thrown their best into the drive on Paris; now they had lost nearly half a million men, and their strength had for a time to be made up of *Landwehr* and *Ersatz* groups. Furthermore—so it was argued—they had intended to sweep the French swiftly from their path, so that then could be released the whole weight of their Army on Russia, held up meanwhile by Austria. This had failed; Schlieffen had failed; moreover the German armies in Poland, instead of occupying Warsaw, were on the verge of being outflanked and were retreating hard from the Vistula. All over the splendid railway systems of Germany men were travelling to and fro, but they were not fighting the enemy in the field, nor training themselves to do so. The Allies had pushed their wedge in between Lille and the sea; doubtless they would force it deeper. Every military expert foresaw the Germans wavering in the West, turning in self-defence to the East.

Instead, the Germans swung without hesitation towards the Channel, and the prize was Antwerp.

Antwerp was the stronghold of Belgium. It was the true left flank of the Allied front, the gateway into the battlefield, a major supply port; its importance was incalculable. The Germans brought to the siege of Antwerp every kind of determination. They forced a passage of the Scheldt at Schoonarde and steadily pressed the Belgians back to cut the main road and rail link between Ghent and Antwerp. To the east they crossed the Nethe. Shortly they were pressing in on all the landward sides of Antwerp, their northern rear protected by the neutrality of Holland. Soon all the forts south of the Nethe were reduced by tremendous shell-fire; the whole defence line fell away. Antwerp prepared for formal siege of an almost mediaeval kind. King Albert left for the village of Selzaete on the Dutch frontier. The hospitals prepared to pack up. The foreign consulates escaped to Ostende. The shops closed. In the trenches outside near Lierre the Belgian infantry, numb and helpless with fatigue, hunched under the continual storm of shrapnel, and often died as they slept.

Just after dark on Monday, 28th September, Antwerp rocked under the first of the 18-inch shells from the Krupp siege guns, throwing projectiles each more than a ton in weight—the "earthquake guns"—and the bombardment began. It was a classic example of invasion by artillery; nothing quite like it had been done before. The shells fell regularly, like the strokes of a great clock, and in the days to come Zeppelins cruised overhead scattering bombs. The inhabitants of the town abandoned it in desperate panic-stricken streams; by and by thousands of them had arrived in the little Dutch town of Roosendaal twenty miles away, where they filled the station in dense, bewildered, weeping crowds.

Mr Winston Churchill had already planned to visit Dunkirk on 3rd October to consult with the Marine Brigade. At eleven on the previous night he was on his way to Dover when his special train suddenly reversed and went back to Victoria. He was urgently asked to see Kitchener in his home in Carlton Gardens. There he found the War Minister with Grey, the First Sea Lord, and Sir William Tyrrell of the Foreign Office. They showed him a telegram the British Minister in Antwerp, Sir Francis Villiers, had filed at eight twenty that evening; it had just been received, at ten. It said in one sentence that the Belgian Government was withdrawing to Ostende, the King was pulling out his field army, and that it was possible that Antwerp might hold out from five to six days more.

This was disastrous news to the War Office, who had not realised the imminence of the danger. Some kind of intervention was immediately necessary to reinforce the disintegrating Belgian garrison. Kitchener decided that the British should send to the rescue if the French would co-operate. Grey at once wired the decision to Paris.

Someone had to go at once to examine the situation on

the spot, and to inform the desperate Belgians that they were not necessarily to be abandoned. Winston Churchill was in any case on his way to Dunkirk; he decided to go instead to Antwerp, and hurried back to his special train. At three the following afternoon he was in Antwerp, and consulted the Belgian Foreign Minister, M. de Broqueville, and General Deguisse, commanding the fortress, as the immense shells thudded into the city around them. They said that the Belgian garrison was almost anaesthetised with fatigue, and was running short even of ammunition. All sense of security had faded from the town, which was already smouldering with rumours and defeatism spread by the German sympathisers of whom more appeared every hour.

On the 4th the British reinforcements arrived: one Marine Brigade and two Naval Brigades, about 8,000 men. The Belgians were too exhausted and discouraged to be much revived. Winston Churchill, as ever, reacted vigorously, almost it seemed eagerly, to the pressure of crisis, sent an urgent telegram to the Prime Minister proposing to resign his office to take over personal command of the British forces around Antwerp. He was, after all, an ex-lieutenant in the Hussars. Mr Asquith, perhaps reflecting that such an appointment would put Mr Churchill in command of two distinguished major-generals and considerable numbers of brigadiers and colonels, wired back that in no circumstances could Mr Churchill be spared from the Admiralty, to which office he should return forthwith. This Mr Churchill did, meeting a certain subsequent ridicule with equanimity. He demanded that the Prime Minister should no longer take a conventional view of his, Mr Churchill's, future, but should relieve him of his office and give him some kind of military command. For a quarter of an hour the First Lord pleaded, argued, protested, stormed with a quite unavailing eloquence; at the end of it he returned to the Admiralty.

Five days later, as dusk fell on Friday the 9th October, the Germans entered Antwerp. They imposed a war levy on the city of £20,000,000. To the Allied command the price seemed even higher; it was the loss of the cornerstone of the entire front.

The situation around the Belgian border was wretched indeed; throughout that autumn the country was gradually torn to pieces. The battlefield, the region bordering on the seaward edge of her western frontier, was unlike the countryside east of Paris, with its gentle hills and broad river valleys. It was densely industrialised, overbuilt, congested, with its agglomerations so close to each other that only the marshes prevented it resembling one sprawling town. Near the coast was the Wattergande, the reclaimed fenland drained by a great tangle of dykes and canals. It was flat, except for a small hill 500 feet high north-east of Hazebrouck, called Mont des Cats, with spurs radiating from it like fingers, and on it stood the town of Cassel. In this blind country the BEF engaged the advance guard of the German cavalry, the *Jäger* and *Schützen* detachments, working their way behind their guns from town to town, village to village, house to house, wall to wall. It was difficult country for artillery, which used every church spire as a range-finding reference. The Germans fortified every building they overran, frequently placing their machine-guns in the middle of rooms, commanding approaches through the windows. The problem of the well-placed machine-gun against infantry in column of route was something no amount of home training could solve; the early losses were grievous. Orders were given that every house be searched, and that no quarter was to be given to any enemy soldier found inside; no prisoners were to be taken in these circumstances.

South of the Lys River the land was soon laid waste: groups of smouldering ruins inhabited by the rotting carcasses of horses, cattle and men. Not a standing tree was left; where wood had been was a wilderness of stumps and roots.

Through this nightmare landscape wandered thousands of drifting and starving Belgians. Thousands more escaped over the border. The phenomenon of the Belgian refugees became the melancholy symbol of this new variety of war. These stricken people streamed away in any direction that was momentarily open. Twenty-five thousand fled to Amsterdam; in the province of Zeeland there were nearly half a million. In small places like Yserduk and Sluis they represented one in three of the population. Tens of thousands straggled along the Flushing coast, completely destitute.

By October there were already 70,000 Belgian refugees

in England, presenting an immense economic and social problem. On their arrival they were dealt with in an improvised fashion by the Local Government Boards in huge institutions like the Alexandra Palace or Earl's Court; they were then passed on to the War Refugees' Committee whose function was to place them, somehow, in private homes; from the start the management of this pitiful and complex human proposition was not a question for the Government at all, and the Local Government authorities seemed mainly preoccupied with a suspicion that somehow the refugees had arrived to complicate the labour market. A statement was in fact issued stating in the most chilling terms: "The War Refugees' Committee desires to protest most emphatically against employment of Refugees in work which might be done by our own people as being always mischievous, at the best thoughtless and at the worst selfish. . . . In general the proper way to relieve Refugees is by gifts and hospitality."

There was a good deal of protest from people who held this to be both churlish and impractical, since the presence of an immobile community at the same time useless and demoralised could be dangerous. Danger, too, was on the mind of the Intelligence and Security forces, who watched the arrival in Folkestone of this unsortable and unidentifiable mass of foreigners with the helpless certainty that at least some of them must be enemy agents.

Already Belgium itself seemed doomed. A breath of what might have been misgiving seemed momentarily to pass over enlightened thought in Germany itself—an article appeared in the *Lokal-Anzeiger* venturing to suggest that some sympathy might be felt for Belgium "tricked and deceived by England." The paper received such a swift rap over the knuckles for this that it instantly recanted, and atoned with an editorial saying that Belgium "has forfeited all right to existence, all claim to share in Germany's magnanimity."

With Antwerp, or rather a couple of days before, fell Arras. This ancient and pleasant town had somehow not realised that it was in the line of operations, until citizens strolling on a hill west of the town saw the Germans encamping on the plain below, and fled, just as the French artillery arrived and the duel began. The story of Arras was the story of so many towns of France and Flanders then: it was surrounded by a double line of fortifications, including the great citadel built by Sebastien Vauban, military engineer to the Grand Monarque in 1669, and ironically called "*La Belle Inutile.*" In a day the Germans commanded them all. The Military Governor ordered all men between eighteen and forty-five out of the town, sheltered the women in cellars; within two hours the Germans had arrived.

Sir John French, obsessed by the danger of the Channel ports, had moved the BEF from the Aisne northwards to the sector of Ypres, on the left of the French line—Ypres, or, as the Flemings called it, Yperen, a quiet and pleasant old township famous over six hundred years for its woolen and linen manufactures. Many tourists had gone out of their way to see its superlative Gothic Cloth Hall, with its forty-four statues of the Counts of Flanders. To the soldiers of the BEF it presented, to begin with, mainly a problem of pronunciation. To some, seeing it for the first time in an autumn evening of 1914, it had a rare and unexpected beauty, haunted for those who knew it with fading ghosts of the Flemish Guilds, of Vauban, of the Duke of Alva. Already its doom was foretold in the lazy puffs of shrapnel over its horizon, but it was ancient and fine. By and by as it was to collapse and disintegrate so was its name; it went down to tradition in the British Army as "Wipers."

Sir John French thought that he could break through at Ypres. The Germans, stimulated and encouraged by the fall of Antwerp, believed they could without difficulty overrun the British, as they were urged by the Order of the Day from the Kaiser's headquarters, in another casual phrase to endure longer than its merits: "The German forces," it said, "will march over Sir John French and his contemptible little army."

At Ypres came the head-on collision. There the fighting lasted off and on for many terrible months; for Ypres saw what was probably one of the bloodiest, longest and most terrible encounters of arms ever recorded in the history of war. Ypres was saved, the road to the Channel ports was barred, at the cost of 50,000 of the most irreplaceable of lives, and the creation of a fearsome salient that embarrassed the British Army for all the years of the war to come, and came near to draining the BEF dry.

But all around lay the sea, the 140,000,000 square miles of ocean of which almost every acre could be considered a potential battlefield, of which indeed the most remote and unexpected areas turned out so to be. At sea Britain felt if not secure, then confident; her forces on land might be small and, as the Kaiser had said, contemptible, but afloat she was well found and well armed. Britain had a naval margin over Germany of 60 per cent in ships and 100 per cent in men. The Admiralty had made a terrible mistake with the *Goeben* and the *Breslau*, to be sure; this was accepted and ruefully written off; nevertheless Beatty's sweep into the Heligoland Bight had shaken the German Fleet so seriously that it must now keep its High Seas units as far as possible out of harm's way. This was a great convenience to the Royal Navy as far as the local seaways were concerned; nevertheless the world was a big place, full of surprises.

At the start of the war the comparative strengths of war vessels were: Britain 679; France 382; Russia 249; Japan 161—a total of 1,471, of which 235 were being built. On the other side the figures were: Germany 369; Austria-Hungary 157; Turkey 22—548 in all, of which about 80 were under construction. Britain had 34 vessels of the Dreadnought class as against 21 owned by Germany; 74 of the pre-Dreadnought class against Germany's 29; 83 cruisers to Germany's 43.

At the outbreak of the War the German Fleet abroad in foreign stations was disposed roughly thus: in the China section were the *Scharnhorst*, the *Gneisenau, Emden, Nürn-*

berg and *Leipzig;* the *Königsberg* was somewhere in the Indian Ocean, off East Africa; the *Dresden* and *Karlsruhe* were about the Caribbean. They were all modern, good warships; moreover there were said to be many fast armed merchantmen. The game began on a vast elastic chessboard with pieces elusive, variable and indeterminate; it was the kind of game wholly suited to the broad sudden gestures of the Winston Churchill technique. In his Admiralty war-room was an immense map, twenty feet high by thirty feet long; it was the task of many junior officers to fill this great flat stage with the positions of all the fighting units of the world, established or speculative. On it, at the start of the war, could be marked the Royal Navy at Hong Kong, the Australians at Sydney, the Germans . . . Admiral von Spee, it was known, was at Panape in the Carolines; the rest were—where? In the centre of Churchill's map was a great blue empty acreage of the Pacific—and the South Atlantic. . . . No one knew anything, for certain. For the first few weeks the pawns were moved obviously and challengingly around; the seas were full of action, ships were sinking others, or being sunk.

Churchill cut the foreign stations to a minimum. By the end of the war's first month he had collected ships from all over the Empire, he had commissioned and armed twenty-four liners as auxiliary cruisers, had defensively armed fifty-four merchantmen, had recommissioned every old and obsolescent naval craft afloat. The 7th Cruiser Squadron remained based on the Nore, to guarantee the North Sea.

The first great obsession was the transport line. The Canadians had to be carried across the Atlantic. The Indians had to be carried across half the world. The Australians had to be borne even farther. . . . The Canadian convoy sailed on 14th October; ten days later it reached Plymouth without loss. Five divisions arrived from India. Two divisions from Australia and New Zealand reached Egypt. There was from beginning to end of that early operation no single accident, the loss of not one life.

In the Pacific, at least, Churchill felt reasonably secure. It was of course infested with islands, but there were no especial bases, and all the German wireless-telegraph stations were put out of commission—in Apia, Yap, Nauru and Rabaul. Then, almost unexpectedly, the Western Allies suddenly were joined by another in Asia: Japan. There had been absolutely no legal reason to invoke her help, and no moral one either as far as anyone knew. Nevertheless Japan abruptly sent an ultimatum to the German Empire demanding her surrender of her base at Tsingtao, on the Shantung peninsula south of the Korean strait. With the German refusal, Japan entered the war. At no time did this make any significant difference to the Allied strategy, but it relieved Mr Churchill's mind vis-à-vis the Pacific, and it added new flags to his enormous map.

The Naval history of those early months fulfils the simple analogy of a monstrous game of chess, in which counter after counter was removed from the board, each piece representing some terribly abrupt and indescribable accumulation of personal destruction. In September the

German cruiser *Hela* was torpedoed by the British submarine E 9; the German cruiser *Cap Trafalgar* was sunk by the British auxiliary *Carmania;* the British cruisers *Aboukir, Cressy* and *Hogue* went down. In October 600 Russians were killed when their cruiser *Pallada* was blown up in the Baltic; 300 Japanese went down with a cruiser mined in Kiaochow Bay. . . . The loss and wastage was fantastic; it seemed that every day many thousands of tons of naval iron and steel and flesh and blood went to the bottom of this ocean or that; and every day too, it seemed, the elusive German cruiser *Emden* appeared in some wildly unexpected corner of the seas between Penang and the Horn. . . . There were occasional individual dramas, only to be recounted months later: the Pacific S. N. Company's liner *Ortega*, for example, was one of the hundreds of merchantmen caught by the outbreak of the war at the other side of the world; she was off Peru and the war already two weeks old before she knew of it at all. At Callao she took aboard 300 Frenchmen to return them for enlistment, and fifty women and children. Off the Chilean coast she sighted the ominous three-funnelled silhouette of the fast cruiser *Dresden*, and ran for it. *Ortega* was unarmed and capable of fourteen or fifteen knots; *Dresden* of twenty. But the German had been long at sea, her bottom was fouled and her speed reduced; the *Ortega's* master, Captain Douglas Kinneir, was able to dodge into the little Nelson Passage, leading to the Magellan Strait, almost unknown to large ships. He manouevred the hundred miles of this channel, almost a creek, preceded by a ship's boat taking soundings all the way, and thus escaped. Captain Kinneir won the DSC, the first war decoration to a merchant seaman.

By the end of October the British Fleet was beginning, as Churchill thought, to have illusions: the Admiralty saw U-Boats everywhere, even in Scapa Flow, which as everyone knew was impregnable. The first sense of security was gone; Admiral Beatty warned Churchill that the Navy now felt no base was wholly safe. Then on the 20th the battleship *Audacious* blew up, supposedly by a torpedo, in Lough Swilly; it was a loss so sensationally serious that the press was asked to say nothing about it. The newspapers took this hardly, insisting that everyone appeared to know all about it anyway, including all the passengers of the *Olympic*, which had passed the stricken battleship, and also without doubt all the German spies in the United Kingdom. . . . For several days much journalistic ingenuity was expended in devising stories in which the word "audacious" should appear, legally lower-case. And yet for some inexplicable reason it was five weeks before the Germans were sure enough of their success to announce it.

On the day the news was published of the combined operation of the Fleet with the Army in Belgium—the sending of the Naval brigades to Antwerp—the *Times* newspaper was especially sardonic about the "amphibious activities" of the Admiralty, suggesting that everyone would be better pleased if the Navy kept to what it called "blue water," and, in particular, disposed of the German cruisers which were harrying British merchant shipping all over the world. There were, indeed, some eight or nine

German cruisers at large in the Atlantic, Pacific and Indian Oceans. More than seventy cruisers—British, French, Russian, Japanese—were systematically hunting for them, and the problem was gigantic, since the oceans were very broad, the islands and neutral havens multitudinous. By October some thirty-nine British merchantmen had been destroyed by these naval francs-tireurs—just under one per cent of the effective total. "There is no occasion for anxiety," said the Admiralty rather stiffly, "and no cause for complaint."

It was simple enough to turn the indictment from the policy to the personality. Mr Churchill, said the *Morning Post*, was a "brilliant and erratic amateur," who had gathered the whole power of the Admiralty into his own hands, meddled in everything, and disregarded all expert advice. This might have been so; it was a question of fact of which no one had any particular knowledge. The *Pall Mall Gazette* hastened to the First Lord's defence, protesting at the "biting at Mr Churchill's heels at this supreme moment when all his energies are engaged on his momentous duties." The *Morning Post* replied by demanding that the professional members of the Board of Admiralty should conduct Naval affairs independently of the First Lord—in other words, said the *Daily News*, negate the constitutional system, substitute the German for the British system, and remove Parliamentary control from naval operations. . . .

Meanwhile, Admiral von Spee roamed the South Atlantic with the *Scharnhorst* and the *Gneisenau*, picking off the British freighters one by one.

Von Spee had sailed from Tsingtao in China at the end of June with *Scharnhorst* and *Gneisenau*. When war began he was near the Solomons; he was then reported off New Guinea, the Carolines, the Solomons. . . . On Churchill's vast war map he appeared as an elusive yet determined pinpoint in the immensity of the Pacific—into which, by and by, he disappeared. It was thought he was heading for the Horn. No one knew. In mid-September Rear-Admiral Cradock, Commander of the South American station, was ordered to find him, if possible, and head him off.

On the 22nd von Spee suddenly appeared out of nowhere, briefly bombarded Papeete in the Society group, and vanished again. On 4th October he was reported between the Marquesas and Easter Island. On the 18th he was heading straight for South America, where the British would surely find him, as he would now have to coal. There, off Coronel in Chile, the long game of hide-and-seek came to an end. Von Spee sighted the cruiser *Glasgow*, and steamed south to head her off.

On the last of the month, a day of great storm, the British cruisers *Glasgow*, *Good Hope*, and *Monmouth* engaged the *Scharnhorst*, *Gneisenau*, *Leipzig* and *Dresden* in what Churchill was later to call "the saddest naval action of all the war." There was no action until sunset, and in all the battle lasted not quite one hour. In the first moments both *Monmouth* and *Good Hope* took fire, but they fought on until dusk, when they were both shelled into a blaze and destroyed, and with them nine out of every ten men aboard, from the Admiral downward.

The Germans had, weight for weight and gun for gun, a superiority of eight to one. They suffered no loss nor casualty at all. Just a month had to pass before their turn was to come, not far away.

As winter began to close in the war was fast developing on lines that Grey and Bethmann-Hollweg and Poincaré had all foreseen and feared: it was becoming a world war. The navies were tensely stretched. They were transporting men and supplies to France, conducting operations against the Belgian coast; they were convoying soldiers from Canada, India and Australia. Moreover, there were no fewer than six major expeditions on the German overseas possessions. (There were many wry ironic comments from the English Tories on the fact that it had taken a Liberal administration to be the first British Government to plan for the seizure of the German colonies.) A British force had attacked Togoland and was moving on the Cameroons. The Australians and New Zealanders were to take Samoa and the German Pacific islands, then New Guinea. An Anglo-Indian force was to attack German East Africa. And now General Botha—ten years before a bitter enemy of the English—was leading an expedition on German South West Africa. Japan had declared war on the Allied side, though that seemed obscure and far away. When at the end of

November Portugal announced her adherence to the Allied cause, it attracted practically no attention at all.

Italy continued to waver, to temporise, to teeter uncertainly between the opposing sides, for neither of which had she any love at all. Austria, to be sure, was her traditional enemy—yet it was France who had robbed her of Tunisia; the urge of self-interest persuaded her that intervention on the winning side would almost certainly lead Italy into the camp of the Powers. The Socialists invoked first the class struggle, then imperialism. The earnest and active thirty-one-year-old radical journalist, Benito Mussolini, first favoured non-intervention, then supported a declaration of war against Austria. Incongruously, indeed fantastically, he drew to his side the new wild man of the Italian arts, the Futurist Filippo Marinetti, who enthusiastically hailed the possibility of war as the complete justification of Futurism itself—war, he proclaimed in a great manifesto, would be the ultimate redemption and release of mankind, eliminating politicians, philosophers, historians, tradesmen, bankers, priests, workers, luxury, poverty, garden cities, aesthetics and much else besides. It was the curious destiny of Filippo Marinetti and Benito Mussolini that they should both be arrested together. Italy, fiddling with the idea of war, could still not make up her mind.

But now a bigger thing came about: Turkey was in the war at last, an open enemy, as had been inevitable from the start, implicit in her secret agreements with Germany. Two months previously when the *Goeben* and *Breslau* had sheltered in Turkish waters, the attitude of the Porte struck the British Admiralty as so impudent and arrogant that the British Naval mission had been withdrawn and the Navy had been patrolling outside the Dardanelles ever since, like incensed detectives without a search-warrant, determined to send the *Goeben* and *Breslau* to the bottom if they came out, whatever flag they happened to be flying at the time.

By mid-October it seemed likely that Turkey was ready to invade Egypt; British outposts beyond the Suez Canal were aware of gathering Turkish forces. Since the defence of Egypt and the Canal was held to be utterly imperative, the British garrison—a Territorial division and Yeomanry regiments sent out at the start of the war to replace the Regulars—was now reinforced with Indian troops, and some Anzac contingents on the way to France were taken off at Port Said.

Then at the end of the month Turkey took the bit between her teeth and shelled the Russian Black Sea ports of Sebastopol, Odessa and Novorossiysk, and the next day the Allies declared war upon her. On the day von Spee was hammering the British cruisers off Coronel, the Navy shelled the Dardanelles and Cap Helles. The French shelled Kum Kale. Every gunner, as he laid his gun on the Turkish coast, wished fervently that it had been the *Goeben* or the *Breslau*.

That November, Britain annexed the island of Cyprus. From 1878, indeed, Cyprus had been administered by Britain, who had occupied the place since the Treaty of Berlin, though it was still considered technically part of the Ottoman Empire, which had only "assigned," and not ceded, the island to Britain. The Turkish entry into the war caused the immediate taking over of Cyprus; eleven years later it was declared a Crown Colony.

By now not only the official belligerents were seriously affected by the spread of the war. For some time the neutral nations had been growing increasingly restive at its interference in their own concerns; particularly was Britain's conduct of the sea-war causing friction. The intensification of the blockade against Germany was causing great inconvenience, exasperation and loss to the trading countries, who protested with growing bitterness as their ships were stopped, searched, and often seized. Finally a State Proclamation had to be issued in the *London Gazette*, with an Order in Council defining what was in fact Britain's relationship with the world, or that part of it with which she was not actively at war.

In this Britain explained that part of the strategy employed against the enemy by virtue of Britain's command of the near seas aimed at preventing Germany obtaining, from any source, supplies useful in prolonging the war. By gradual extension of definitions, that in effect meant anything at all. The Naval Conference in the summer had drawn up the Declaration of London, which was supposed to codify the rules for this sort of operation. Among other things it divided contraband into two classes: "absolute," or goods which by their very character were destined for war use, and "conditional," those which not necessarily designed for war use could in some circumstances be put to that use. In addition it listed commodities which in no circumstances could be treated as contraband at all.

The trouble with the Declaration of London was that it was ratified by nobody at all, and was therefore not legally binding, and even if it had been there was no one in a position to see the rules were kept. Britain, however, announced that she had adopted it, subject to certain modifications. These modifications, it was claimed by aggrieved neutrals, merely removed the rules altogether. In the first place she had added to the contraband list many commodities defined by the Declaration as free—arguing that minerals could be made into shells, and hides could be made into boots—and amended the article that said "conditional" contraband could not be seized unless it was to be landed in an enemy port. Britain now declared her intention to seize ships carrying such cargoes to neutral ports, or even on their way home from such ports. Britain made it clear that she had no intention of allowing Germany to get through Rotterdam the goods she could not land at her own ports. Moreover, it was added, while Britain did not wish to interfere with legal trade between neutral countries, she could not allow Germany to be supplied with useful material under cover of such neutral trade.

There was a great deal of protest from Holland, whose hard case was especially clear, and from Sweden, whose iron-ore trade with Germany was an almost indispensable part of her commerce. The United States in particular made bitter complaints; her business men foresaw the loss of their entire trade with Holland and Denmark and, of course, Germany. Britain was suddenly startled by the vigour of the official United States Note that Mr Bryan, the Secretary of State, despatched to the British Government, protesting at the "grievous disabilities inflicted on US industry—an unwarranted interference in US trade." Washington warned London that "much feeling was aroused" in America, whose industrialists "held Britain responsible for the depression existing in many US industries."

Sir Cecil Spring-Rice, Britain's Ambassador to the United States, did his best to soothe the Americans while maintaining the propriety of Britain's case and her determination to pursue her methods. He pointed out that the demand in Europe at the time for food, clothing and military supplies had already brought nearly £15,000,000 worth of new export business a week to American industries. He was told in turn that only Britain's "unjust attitude" prevented that figure being doubled.

That week a premium of fifteen guineas percent was being laid in Lloyds on policies worded: "To pay a total loss in the event of a declaration of war between Great Britain and America within twelve months." (This was exactly twice the premium demanded against a similar declaration between Britain and Norway.)

For some time the German propaganda machine in America found its task sensibly easier. America had, after all, its 18,000,000 citizens still speaking German as a first language, its considerable population of irreconcilable Irishmen. In the autumn a letter was sent to the Irish press from

New York by Sir Roger Casement. He had been eighteen years a British Consul until his resignation in 1913; he was now a militant Nationalist. "Before God and man," he wrote, "Germany has never wronged Ireland, and we owe her more than one debt of gratitude." Shortly afterwards the *Norddeutsche Allgemeine Zeitung*, the organ of the German Foreign Office, reported that Casement had arrived in Berlin and had been received, not surprisingly, with cordiality. He had requested, and obtained, an assurance that Germany had no designs upon Ireland. . . . Yet fundamentally the United States, and certainly the United States Government, was both logically and emotionally disposed to support the Allied cause, and the savage cartoons of the American newspapers poured more abuse on the Kaiser almost than did the British. President Wilson nominated a national day "of prayer and supplication for peace and concord throughout the world." In his address to Congress he insisted that the United States stood aside from the conflict only in the hope that she might counsel peace. It would be a great loss, said the President, if America lost her reputation as a potential mediator.

Meanwhile American commercial men continued to move in and out of Germany, at increasing risk to themselves, and indeed equally in and out of France and Britain.

Jerome K. Jerome, travelling on a transatlantic liner to New York, wrote home:

> One delightful fellow that I chatted with was the proprietor of a quick-firing gun which he had succeeded in selling to the Belgians. He was highly pleased with its success. Properly handled, and with opportunity, it can be

worked for sixty hours at a stretch, mowing down its men without intermission. A picturesque account of the slaughter it had accomplished in one battle he had telegraphed from Belgium to his firm in America. It had so upset the inventor of the gun, a mild and humane gentleman by nature, that he had shut himself up in his house, a prey to remorse. I left the proprietor of the gun making a collection for the wounded.

During that autumn the Germans had massed four cavalry corps and two armies between the Lys and the sea —altogether fifteen army corps, under the Crown Prince of Bavaria, Generals Fabech and Deimling, and the Duke of Württemberg. The Belgian Army had emerged from Antwerp more or less intact, but exhausted to the point where it was incapable of action. The British left their front on the Aisne and moved north. The left of General Castelnau's Army did not extend beyond the south of Arras; from there to the south of Lille it was taken over by General de Maud'huy's Army. It was enough to allow General Foch, who had been called by Joffre to command the armies in the north, to hold the Germans. Their attack had tended at first towards taking Dunkirk and thus reaching Calais—all the heavy artillery used at Antwerp had been brought forward; the censor released a picture of an enormous cannon made by Krupp, mounted on a twenty-four-wheeled railcar and said to be the biggest gun in the world.

But early in November the attack was held, the Germans rocked backwards, with their great artillery sinking into the mud, and the BEF went on towards the Yser, and to the furious and terrible battle at Ypres.

The Germans lost 120,000 men.

The damp browns of autumn faded into the grey of winter, into the iron-coloured pitiless chill of late November, and slowly it seemed as though something of that unmerciful cold had petrified the war itself, which slowly as the days went on ground to a standstill, with many hundreds of thousands of men gradually, purposefully, anxiously, bitterly digging themselves into the soil of Europe, burying themselves below the surface as efficiently as might be; huge armies entrenching themselves in fields and roadsides as though they were to be there for years. There seemed no alternative now to a war of attrition on the Western Front that might go on for months, years, generations, forever.

Trench warfare was a comparatively new conception; the equipoise of two immense forces made it inevitable; as winter trod numbly over northern Europe the troops dug in like engineering moles; by and by there were trenches almost all the way from Switzerland to the sea. These were not at all in groups of isolated rifle-pits, as had been known before, but like many series of small towns linked by narrow communicating trenches, each battalion occupying one little community which might stretch anywhere from half a mile to two miles long, and a hundred yards deep. Behind the firing trenches were labyrinths of intersecting support trenches, communication trenches, dugouts for the staff, offices, kitchens: the whole thing might take half an hour to go through.

For military strategists there was the phenomenon of

the frontal attack. This was a thing that had not been seen in large-scale warfare for a generation. All wars of comparatively recent times had involved sweeps, wide turning movements, the covering of country. So it had been with the Franco-Prussian war, the Russo-Japanese war. But now, in France and Flanders, war had petrified. There were no longer any flanks to turn, and any turning movement must be of such a size that it would resemble a separate war. There was no longer anywhere to move to. There was no longer any cavalry function. Armies of a size unknown before were frozen into a posture face to face—and almost literally in many cases; close quarters meant trenches separated not by miles or even a mile, not half a mile apart nor sometimes not yet a hundred yards; in parts of the Ypres sector the front-line trenches were seventy feet from one another. It became a war where surprise could scarcely be invoked even tactically. Barbed wire needs artillery barrages to break it down; enormous preparations for a movement involving an advance to be measured in yards. So began the war of exhaustion.

The early news from the Polish front had been encouraging; it was said that in the battle for Warsaw the Germans were failing. They had indeed to fight bitterly, their flanks enclosed by great rivers. Across the sixty-mile gap between Plotsk on the Vistula and Unieyev on the Warta the armies beat and pressed against each other; it was impossible for either to outflank the other; they were wedged. The British censor permitted the publication of enthusiastic prophecies of a German rout.

Yet in the fact, the Russians had throughout been wholly unequal to the Germans either in discipline or skill. The twenty cavalry and infantry divisions of Rennenkampf, the fifteen divisions of Samsonoff—faced by fifteen German divisions under Hindenburg and Ludendorff they had fallen to pieces. The Russian armies came to an end at the defeats of Tannenberg and the Masurian Lakes, with the fantastic loss of more than 100,000 men, driven back to the Bzura-Ravka River before Warsaw.

In just over two weeks Hindenburg and Ludendorff smashed two great Russian armies, each alone greater than all of theirs. Yet the Russians continued somehow to press against the Austria-Hungarian armies in Galicia. They won the Battle of Lemberg, and England—made loudly aware of this alone—applauded, wholly overlooking the disasters of Tannenberg.

Russia had begun her war with about 5,000 guns and 5,000,000 shells. In the first three months she had fired some 45,000 shells a day—while manufacturing for her resources about 35,000 a month. It was not long before the Czarist armies had hardly a week's shell-reserve left; they had lost more than 1,000,000 rifles; by the end of the year more than 1,350,000 Russians were killed, wounded or captive. To be sure there were drafts of 800,000 men waiting to replace them, but there was no equipment. All this was dutifully reported to London by the British liaison agent at the Russian HQ, Colonel Knox, who defied the arguments of the Russian War Minister General Sukhomlinoff. It looked increasingly as though Russia must collapse, especially since the entry of Turkey had created for Russia a second front in the Caucasus.

Yet Russia had one immeasurable asset, shared by no other European country: she had endless *land*. It was argued that the Russians would do now exactly as they had done in 1812: withdraw, lure the invaders into huge and terrible traps.

One man maintained his vehement approach, half theatrical and half practical: Mr Winston Churchill, insisting on comparing the immense Allied front, now from the Aegean to the North Sea, as the simple holding of an "isthmus." It consoled nobody.

On the Western Front, trench warfare itself, merely by definition, brought about a terrible sort of stagnation. For a year or more, or until all the regular officers trained in the old methods had themselves been killed, the feeling existed among the professional military that this grim and hopeless immobility was in some obscure way due to a lack of human qualities—even, perhaps, discipline. After all—it was sometimes argued—the only way the Germans could repel an attack was by shooting, and in order to shoot they must expose themselves, and could therefore be shot at. Many memories still lingered of the old Boer sharpshooters: the invincible Voertrekker marksmen. If such a company could be there to provide an attack with covering fire, could any German defence be able to man its trenches? No man in trench warfare could possibly get into position, locate his target, aim and fire in under twenty seconds, during which time he would surely have been hit himself. Theoretically, then, expert infantry could cross any no-man's-land and cut through the wire without excessive loss. Practically, of course, it never happened, since the entire responsibility for gaining fire power had been handed over to the artillery; the infantry merely groped along in the wake of the shells. And every intelligent officer knew perfectly well why this was: it was the imponderable factor of fear. No soldier at the front could possibly behave like a soldier on manoeuvre and take careful aim when nine-tenths of his psychological forces were concentrated on mastering his personal terror of mechanical noisy death. Someone else had to do the laying of guns, the aiming and the shooting, and that must be someone himself insulated from the whine of bullets round his ears—the gunners in the rear. The trouble with this was that the infantryman, relieved of his technical initiative, merely had more time in which to reflect on his personal danger, and this was a mood profoundly encouraged by the trenches. Trenches were a protection to the soldier only for so long as he was not in fact fighting. The first head over the parapet was there to be shot off; moreover a skilfully-placed traversing machine-gun could mow down an entire line of entrenched men. The trench was the protection against artillery fire—and that brought the problem round full circle. From the beginning of trench warfare to its end, there remained the one recurrent horrifying climax of every action, the repetitive moment of truth, which was Going Over the Top.

On the quiet days there were snipers, and the endless

task of repairing the trench itself, thickening the breast-work, shoring up the dugout, replacing the duckboard, improvising fireplaces from the tin linings of ammunition boxes with chimneys of bully-beef cans. The cold grew worse, so bad that the water froze in the cooling-jackets of the machine-guns; sometimes a frozen rifle-barrel ruptured at the sudden expansion on being fired; and men became so rigid with the cold that occasionally they had to be physically lifted from their post on relief. They huddled in their "comforters," wrapped straw round their legs, stuffed their tunics with newspapers. Some fortunate units got an issue of goatskin capes. And outside, between the lines, among the muck and the wire and the lunar landscape of no-man's-land, there was death, obtruding on all the senses.

Most men submitted, since there was indeed nothing else to do; only a few left something of their personal trauma on the records in writing and verse, endeavouring to exercise something of the horror by expressing it horribly, defining with irony the pain of fear and despair—like E. Wyndham Tennant, three months before his own death:

> . . . Can't you see
> When the flare goes up? Sh, boys; what's the noise?
> Do you know what those rats eat? Body-meat!

—all in a tormented effort to drive the wretchedness into the open.

Down from the Channel to the heart of Europe men were scraping and scratching and burrowing and watching and flinching, huddling at the trench bottom or building up the firestep—for when the firestep was too low all shooting went too high—and for many nights nothing was to be seen of war but the lines of Very lights arcing into the sky, bursting in a moment's metallic brilliance, fading out, reappearing; then the Minnenwerfer mortar-bombs, coughing and wobbling across the gap. German artillery was identified onomatopoeically, as Umpahs, Umpies, Pipsqueaks and Bolas. What was happening elsewhere no one knew, nor had much energy to care. During that winter when the trenches approached each other so nearly that a man could throw a packet of tobacco from one front into another—and, in those days, often did—the Germans would run up posters on poles: "Warsaw is taken!" or "Lemberg is ours!" The tales were rejected in the Daily Intelligence Report, which was known as "Comic Cuts"; everything good or bad was received in an accepted mood of suspended judgment, tinged with scepticism. Nothing mattered but that the rations should arrive, that one's turn to go back into support should not be deferred by sudden action, that the rain might stop and the cold might abate.

On one French sector the enemies confronted each other so intimately that a strange *modus vivendi* was evolved. The fantasy of the situation was emphasised by the fact that there was only one source of water for both sides, a small well beside a deserted millhouse halfway between the lines, and a form of tacit agreement came about that French and Germans should use it alternately. One day the French party found beside the well a bundle of recent German newspapers; they took them, replaced them with French papers. Next day these had disappeared. The exchange went on for a week. Meanwhile the formalities of warfare were maintained: the French were building a support fortification and the Germans reinforcing a redoubt; each day each side destroyed the work of the other, and each night the construction was repaired.

After another week of this routine two German officers left their trenches unarmed and with raised hands, walked across to the French lines and, calling on the French infantry officers, pointed out that this procedure was mutually fruitless, exasperating and wasteful, and proposed that since conditions were troublesome enough in any case they need not be aggravated by unnecessary strife. The French agreed to a mutual respect for each side's fortifications. A curious relationship developed, to the point where very soon the opposing soldiers were sharing tobacco with each other, and even taking coffee with each other round the well.

This endured until the day came when the Germans informed the French that they, who were Bavarians, were about to be relieved. If the relief were to be a Prussian unit, said the Bavarians regretfully, it was improbable that this convenient system would continue; in such an event they undertook to leave a warning by hanging pieces of paper on their wire. This they duly did. The following day a thoughtless French water-party was mown down by machine-gun fire, and the war began again.

Overhead there developed a phenomenon that itself marked out this war from any other: men were fighting in the air. One grew accustomed to the spectacle, as one grew accustomed to so many unprecedented and generally sinister things; nevertheless it had never significantly happened before.

To begin with the aeroplane was an erratic toy, most effectively used as a scout, an artillery spotter or observer, flying low among the rifle-bullets and returning to base with news of the enemy dispositions. Sometimes it was more ambitious. Quite early in October the Admiralty announced that there had been "an aerial invasion of Germany by British aviators." Squadron-Commander Spencer Grey RN with two lieutenants had flown to Düsseldorf and thrown several bombs on an aircraft shed, setting a Zeppelin dirigible on fire. "The feat," said the Admiralty, "would appear to be in every way remarkable, having regard to the distance—over one hundred miles—penetrated into enemy territory."

It was only some two months, after all, since the Norwegian Lieutenant Trygve Gran had made the first historic crossing of the North Sea by aeroplane.

Three days later the Germans replied by sending two Taubes over Paris. They dropped small bombs around the Opera, in the rue Montmartre, rue Lafayette, rue de la Banque, the place de la Republique. Three people were killed. One bomb fell on the terrace of Notre Dame, but it bounced away without exploding.

The coastal towns of Dunkirk and Calais saw a German

plane every day, so regularly that "half past three" was known as "*Taube et demie*." It would appear, drop a bomb or two, break some glass, kill one or two people, and go away.

Over the line itself the aeroplanes met in single combat or in groups, and the science of aerial battle was born. In the skies of northern France Fokkers met Farmans, Sopwiths met Taubes, roaring little instruments of fretwork and piano-wire; there among the clouds they manouevred like terriers, weaving and circling at seventy and even eighty miles an hour. It was greatly improvised—the aviators actually duelled with rifles, or even pistols; sometimes a carbine was fixed by an attachment to the side of the cockpit, where the pilot could reach it. . . .

The first echelon of the Royal Flying Corps had not been slow to move into action; it had embarked from Southampton on 11th August, for its forward base at Amiens, under the command of Brigadier General Sir David Henderson, Director of Military Aeronautics, the first man to lead an aerial force into a major war. He had, to begin with, a total uniformed strength of his RFC of 2,073 men. He had an organisation only two years old, and 130 aeroplanes. (France had 500, Germany 470, even Austria had 120. Germany was known also to have two dozen important lighter-than-air flying machines, of which some twenty were to the design of the Graf Zeppelin; they were unknown quantities.)

The observer of one Naval aeroplane won a momentary renown by effecting the extraordinary feat of changing a propeller-blade two thousand feet above the Channel.

From time to time spies were deposited behind the enemy lines on both sides, and, less frequently, collected. An increase in aerial activity generally revived the stories, always current among the ground troops, of enemy agents in their midst. Somebody had recalled what Frederick the Great said: "When Marshal Soubise goes to war he is followed by a hundred cooks—when I take the field I am preceded by a hundred spies." In the forward areas of northern France agents were thought, perhaps rightly, to abound—flashing lights at night, emitting puffs of smoke by day, affecting to be labourers working the fields, disguised as refugees, above all making use of church towers, the hands of whose clocks they could manipulate as semaphores. The German aircraft were often held to be a more mobile and impudent version of the same thing, and whenever a Taube was intercepted overhead the ensuing dogfight was watched with huge partisan enthusiasm.

Sometimes they were worse than a diversion. The time came when a device was invented that showered arrows from the air—sharp and heavy steel darts that were released in fusillades from low-flying aeroplanes; they were packed in cans of heavy oil, and if the dart did not brain the infantryman the oil caused a poisonous wound. . . . The Germans were also said to drop what were called "incendiary discs"—small circles the size of a sixpence, which burned furiously. . . .

It was about this time, though not wholly for this reason, that the French infantry devised a sort of metal skull-cap to be worn under the felt kepi. By and by the

British produced a steel helmet; it was accepted reluctantly, even derisively; it was finally sanctified by a black-and-white artist called Bruce Bairnsfather, who had invented a strange, philosophical, whiskered archetype for the middle-aged Tommy whom he called "Old Bill." . . .

The *London Gazette* of November 24th announced that 2nd Lieutenant His Royal Highness Edward A. C. G. A. P. D., Prince of Wales and Duke of Cornwall, K.G., had been seconded from the Grenadier Guards for service on the Staff. (His younger brother Prince Albert was commissioned in the Navy with the 1st Battle Squadron.) That week secret preparations were made for their father's visit to the British troops in France.

The King arrived at Hazebrouck at half-past nine on the morning of Thursday, 3rd December. It was the first appearance of a British sovereign at a war since 1743, when George II with his Anglo-German Army had defeated the French under Marshal Noailles at Dettingen. A sullen and dismal rain was falling; the King was taken therefore to the only covered area available, which was the railway station, and there he presented several DSOs. He stamped around with an expression of exasperated concern that was recorded forever on the official photographs, a short bowed figure in British Warm and tall boots.

The next day Haig dined with the King at Saint-Omer, in company with Lord Stamfordham, the King's Private Secretary, and his assistant Colonel Clive Wigram, the Prince of Wales, Sir John French and Major-General Wilson. The encounter produced some unusual reflections in Haig all of which he wrote down later—the King was most affable and charming, but full of strange and remote illusions about the nature of soldiers. To King George all serving soldiers were inevitably and by nature "brave"; that was their condition; he was unaware of the elusive quality known as *morale* and could therefore not begin to appreciate the subtle values associated with it. The importance of training he could understand, in a technical sense; it had never occurred to him that there could be corporate psychological factors thereby induced; he had no grasp of imponderables. When Haig described to him the shattering effects of the Ypres fighting on the human material of the Army—how the fugitives swarmed down the Menin Road abandoning everything they carried, throwing away on the roadside even their rifles and their packs, desperate in terror—the King (according to Haig's recollection) expressed himself as saying that this was "interesting."

The King then said that the Victoria Cross was reasonably to be awarded to any soldier carrying a wounded man out of action. Haig protested that every example must necessarily be judged on its individual merits—frequently an ill-considered or careless rescue could actually damage a wounded man; furthermore great precautions had to be taken in battle actually to limit these deeds of heroism; men had to be posted at the front to see that too many unwounded men did not escort casualties from the firing-line. It was a pragmatic approach that had not before occurred to the King.

... 12

To Mr Asquith, in London, the whole situation began to assume an aspect of deep frustration and unhappiness, for which the word nightmare would be too urgent and the word concern too slight. He was baffled and harried at the same time; there were times when he found even the façade of optimism a strain. The Prime Minister now saw the war as an immense equation of innumerable and largely irreconcilable factors: the Allies, with whom he felt little or nothing in common, yet who were forever making extreme and passionate demands, usually unanswerable; there was the British public, depressed and exasperated, solving its frustrations by a steady pressure of criticism of the conduct of the war. Nobody at home, it seemed, really knew anything whatever about the war. The censorship had seen to that, to be sure; the press was increasingly sour about the methods of Sir Stanley Buckmaster. Towards the end of November the French issued an ample, detailed, and on the whole illuminating statement of the events of the previous six weeks; it was published wholly in the *Bulletin des Armées,* and thereafter in all the French press. For the

British version the censor cut all those sections dealing with the affairs of the British Army. The press protested: since the facts had already been printed throughout France they were presumably accessible to the enemy; in any case they dealt with affairs both obvious and bloody of which the enemy was clearly only too aware. Why must the British be insulated from the Commander-in-Chief's assessment of their soldiers' performance, especially since, as everyone knew, it happened to be in this case uncritically complimentary? The censor remained consistent, and said nothing.

Practically nobody in the British administration, with the exception of Lord Kitchener, had ever expected that this war could possibly last more than six months, even at the most pessimistic estimate. After the successes of the Marne multitudes of people, both in Government and out, confidently expected a victory both glorious and comparatively swift. The weeks passed and the hopes faded. The efficiency of the opposing military machines—their immensity, their proficiency at their wretched business—was clearly going to prevent victory or defeat alike. Two huge and almost equivalent masses were clearly settling down to a war of time—worse than a war of time, a war of exhaustion that was nevertheless a war of pain and force, since the cost in blood was horrifying.

Mr Asquith, then, spent his days trying to compose the ragged differences between the soldiers and the politicians. With the company of accomplished and incompatible individualists he had to deal with, his problem was more intricate even than that: the differences grew between politicians and politicians, soldiers and soldiers. Chiefly he had to mediate between Westminster and the Front. Lloyd George especially was vividly impatient with military men and military minds. When the Marne produced no visibly triumphant end to the war he began to complain loudly of regimental ineptitude; he was not easy to assuage. Winston Churchill complained on the other hand of military feebleness, lack of ingenious adventure and resource; he was forever full of plans for complicated amphibious diversions; he paced about the Admiralty consumed with frustrations.

Sir John French suddenly charged the Government and Kitchener with deliberate and criminal apathy in the supply of munitions. The Prime Minister denied this, but the disquiet grew, which could not be publicly revealed.

Great temperamental and practical differences grew between Asquith and Lloyd George—between the discreet and careful Asquith, who had built his career on the principle that results were best achieved by rationalisation and argument and not by rhetoric; Lloyd George who was certain—and was encouraged by Lord Northcliffe in his certainty—that it was perpetually necessary to whip a public up, to agitate, to inspire, to impart to the people the sense of terrible necessity and peril with which he constantly lived himself. Lloyd George was not obsessed and reflective and patient like Asquith; he was volatile and imaginative and, indeed, shrill; he lived on stratagems. Asquith was, as they used to say, the man of excruciating moderation.

When the Army was exposed to criticism he held it to be unjust or ill-informed, as frequently it was, and protected the Army. He was also indeed slow to excite. When he was told, that autumn, that Sir John French was highly sanguine about the next developments on the battlefield, Asquith said that "it was an excellent thing to have an optimist at the front, provided there was a good pessimist at the rear."

Perhaps Lloyd George had been right; here and there the public zeal was manifestly flagging, its spirits drooping as the winter advanced. *Morale*, as it was now called, was reasonably high on the national or official level; yet every day the casualty lists grew longer in finer and finer type.

Out of all this began to develop two parallel and contrasting moods, for the loud motif of angry patriotism was touched here and there, in doubting quarters, with questions sometimes sincere and sometimes cynical. What indeed, as it was occasionally asked, was one in fact fighting for? Germany had not made war on Britain. The country was not threatened. Britain had nothing to gain from the war except the moderation of Germany's arrogance: was that cause enough, in view of the irretrievable loss in men and money? Had Germany committed any specific outrage on Britain that the British were burning to avenge? In principle Britain had gone to war because Germany had invaded Belgium; yet all expert opinion must have been persuaded for years that if Germany ever fought France (and how many had privately approved of that?) she could do no other than begin by invading Belgium.

Yet the pervasive mood was not this by any means, but something very uncomplicated and readily responsive to the elementary emotive calls. It was symbolised by a long and exalted poem apostrophising the Kaiser; it was widely quoted, and studded with passionate marks of exclamation; furthermore its author bore the resounding name of Mohun Ashfordby-Trenchard. Its last verse ran:

> Madman! Ye have not heeded
> The Warning that we gave!
> The sacred soil of France is torn;
> Belgium is in her grave!
> And now *your* doom has fallen!
> Now sets your bloodstained star.
> Now guard ye well, for ye have waked
> The English Race to war!

Yet the other mood was growing too; out of the growing fatigue and helplessness and frustration there developed in some quarters a curious spirit of questioning and doubt, a consciousness of a social disruption long foreseen. Wells had expressed it long before in a spirit of scientific curiosity; Anatole France in a spirit of cynical pity. Now it found its testament in a long and widely-read set of articles in the *News* by A. G. Gardiner, expressing a sense of simultaneous inadequacy and foreboding.

> We invent a vessel to swim beneath the sea and at once it is appropriated to increase the terrors of war. We learn to fly like the birds, and at once flying becomes a new arm of military service, and has little other meaning. We invent new explosives to blast rocks, and we use them to

blast lives. And Mr. Nobel in a spirit of post-mortem peni-
tence leaves posterity a prize for ingeminating peace. . . .

He, and many others, continually quoted Ruskin:
"Competition and anarchy are in all things the law of death."
They brooded on the only too manifest and wanton squan-
dering of life that was going on a couple of hundred miles
away; they brooded on the armaments industry.

> The soldier who has the luck to come out of the war
> alive, [said A.G.G.] will emerge as poor as he went in, but
> the shareholders of Krupps and Armstrongs and Schneiders
> will have the wealth of the Indies as their reward. . . .
> And behind them are the powerful, antisocial elements
> bound up with the Army. Only a few months ago the
> aristocracy revealed the ultimate source of its arrogant
> claims over the democracy. It openly challenged Parlia-
> ment with the threat of the Army. We must expect to find
> that challenge more defiant after the war.

It is true that there were grounds for this disquiet.
Only that week, in October, there appeared a translation of
a book by a French priest, the Abbé Dimnet, eulogising
the doctrine of Treitschke as to the medicinal virtues of
war: the fruit that was to be plucked from the defeat of
Germany was the equal defeat of Republican France and
the restoration of Monarchy and Clericalism to power.
Simultaneously the *Morning Post*, which had no affection
for Asquith's Government and was at no pains to dissimu-
late, said "War will endure as long as human nature," and
scoffed at the words "war to end war." It had apparently
no objection to Bethmann-Hollweg's "scrap of paper,"

since it suggested that Britain should herself "hack her way" through treaties affecting, for example, neutrals. This, the old Liberals deduced, was behind the Tory attacks on Winston Churchill, which indeed were growing: his offence was to be a civilian in charge of the Navy, representing Parliament rather than the service. Very soon the Liberals had detected in the machinery of the Tory press a siege against Parliament itself.

As the winter moved sullenly in and the war settled down like a wasting disease over Europe the mood of the Liberal editorialists became increasingly bitter and introspective and, it seems now, oddly philosophical and objective about the whole mystique of moral values involved. "It is the *insanity* of the thing against which the mind rebels. We labour through generations to build up an elaborate and complex structure of social life and international relationships and then suddenly, at the inspiration of a few despots and diplomatists, the guns of Krupp and Armstrong are brought in to batter the whole thing into a rubbish-heap. No one supposes that the result has anything to do with justice. The moral effect of a good cause, no doubt, is an important factor. But what army ever went into battle believing that it had a bad cause?"

There was, for a day or two, a curious and almost shamefaced reaction among some circles in England when it was reported—falsely, as it turned out—that Fritz Kreisler, fighting for the Austrians, had been wounded in the right arm. The anti-militarists invoked this as a telling symbol of wastage and futility.

There were many groping thoughts and plans for the future . . . "We shall have achieved nothing if we destroy the idol of militarism in Germany without taking care that it is not erected elsewhere. . . . Let us admit that we have done nothing until we have done everything—that war will remain so long as war preparations are permitted. It is useless to talk of separate disarmament. . . ."

In the American *Outlook* appeared an article by Theodore Roosevelt, himself scarcely in any sense a pacifist, who nevertheless argued that neither civilisation nor liberty could exist in existing conditions, and called for the creation of an "international organisation" and a "World Police, that could back righteousness by force." He urged an "agreement between nations that would, having defined the inalienable rights of each, provide that any cause of difference should be submitted to an international court. To supplement and make this effectual," wrote Roosevelt, "it should be solemnly covenanted that if any nation refused to abide by the decision of such a court the others would draw the sword on behalf of peace and justice and would unitedly coerce the recalcitrant nation."

This was read tolerantly and with few philosophical sighs; it was a fanciful notion.

Behind all of Asquith's preoccupations, and in many ways worse than any of them, lurking in the background as the interminable local theme, was the Irish question, nagging and dragging and worrying on Asquith's mind like an incurably aching tooth. War or no war, it was perpetually neccessary to consider bringing the Parties to some accommodation over the Home Rule Bill. Mr Asquith had allowed himself to hope that the unexpected rallying of the Irish Nationalists to the British patriotic cause would in some degree mellow the Unionists and persuade them to accept some settlement acceptable for when at last peace might return. But the Unionists were not to be diverted; they insisted that the Home Rule Bill must be resubmitted after the War to whatever Parliament might be in office. To this the Irish responded by saying that they would surely be worse off then than if no war had happened.

Northern France and Flanders rocked and burned and settled in to an apparently interminable decay, and that great proportion of British male citizens that was later to be known as "the flower of her manhood" suffered and died in conditions of most unsubtle hardship, but the Irish Question went on and on.

"The Irish on both sides are giving me a lot of trouble," said Mr Asquith to his diary, "just at a difficult moment. I sometimes wish we could submerge the whole lot of them and their island for, say, ten years under the waves of the Atlantic."

King George, himself beset by what he held to be local difficulties of an exasperatingly trivial kind, offered himself as a mediator in any way that might be both Constitutional and helpful, commenting acidly on the obsessions of politicians who could wrangle forever through an emergency of such peril. At the slightest sign of any accommodation, said the King, "that old bother about Tyrone and those infernal snippets of Fermanagh and Derry pop up again."

The Irish Bill, with the Welsh Disestablishment Bill, had now to be placed on the Statute Book under the Parliament Act, with a Suspensory Bill deferring their operation for twelve months (or a later date to be fixed by Order in Council) if the war was not yet over. It was pledged on behalf of the Government that before the Irish Bill came into operation Parliament would be given the opportunity to debate and, if necessary, amend it, and that the Government would in no way countenance the use of force to coerce the will of Ulster.

The Suspensory Bill was passed in a sitting, though Bonar Law made a bitter speech in which he flung back at the Prime Minister that passage in his own speech at the start of the war in which he had accused the Germans of bad faith. It seemed as though in Parliament as in France a no-man's-land had grown between the trenches; Government and Opposition stared at each other as though through the wire.

Furthermore the war was now running into realms of almost incomprehensible extent. On 16th November the Prime Minister asked the House of Commons to vote a credit of £225,000,000 "to carry on the war" (in addition to the £100,000,000 previously voted in August). The war, said Mr Asquith, in its first 105 days had cost rather more than £1,000,000 a day, or some ten guineas a second. The vote included £30,250,000 for the Dominions, who wanted to renew certain loans by means of the London money market. One by one the Allies came to Britain, who was defined by everyone as the richest of the Powers. The French asked for a loan of £8,000,000 at 5 per cent—this struck Mr Asquith as being a singular sum, since it represented the cost of the war for about a week. The Cabinet, however, had agreed, on condition that the money was spent on supplies from Britain. Russia wanted to raise £100,000,000—Britain agreed to offer £40,000,000 on condition that 25 per cent of that value in gold be deposited in London. £7,000,000 was lent interest-free to Belgium until the end of the war. There was £800,000 on the same terms to Serbia.

The Napoleonic Wars had left Britain with a debt of £875,000,000 which after a century of economy had remained only slightly reduced when the war began. The Boer War had cost £250,000,000, of which £150,000,000 was met by borrowing, £100,000,000 by taxation. Now Britain, in November 1914, was required by a Cabinet decision to impress on the Allies that she was already spending significantly more on the war than either France or Russia, neither of whom was spending as much as £40,000,000, against Britain's £45,000,000.

Mr Lloyd George's Budget of 17th November was Draconian: it raised income tax from ninepence in the pound earned to a shilling, and from one and threepence to one and eightpence unearned. Beer went up a penny a pint to 5d. The tea duty was brought from fivepence to eightpence a pound. A War Loan of £350,000,000 was issued at 95, bearing interest at 3½ per cent. All the new taxes would bring in only some £65,000,000. There was no keeping pace at all.

The civilian mind, appalled by this incomprehensible extravagance, unable to grasp the fantastic principles of military expenditure on such a scale, yet persuaded that in some way it could be translated into reasonable terms, began to express its exasperation with such details of wastefulness as it could actually see. For a time public criticism shifted from the Spy to the Profiteer, and his abettor the spendthrift bureaucrat. There had been some well-established prototype transactions during the Boer War—the body-belts that were bought by the War Office at 20s 11d a dozen, sold by the War Office for 4s a dozen, bought by a perceptive middleman for 6s 9d and offered back to the military at 18s. It was too soon to uncover what similar deals were going on at the present time; nevertheless there were already many alarming stories from the front of shoddy uniforms that rotted and fell to rags in a matter of weeks, of Army boots that quickly collapsed in the mud of the trenches, of Army huts decaying already through jerry-building.

A Committee on Garrison and Regimental Institutes urged that a central board be quickly formed to control prices and contracts. Evidence was produced that a carefully-organised ring existed to maintain against the War Office a price for iron sheets, for example, some 8 per cent higher than the market quotation.

From the opposite point of view, too, the Authorities

were charged with wastefulness; while the soldier was victimised with inadequate care at the front, he was costing too much money at home. The billeting system—for by now soldiers were boarded out at Government expense in private homes all over Britain—was paradoxically assailed by the spokesmen of civilians who argued they were being paid too highly. The War Office provided for a reimbursement of 3s 4½d a day for the billeting of one H. M. armed forces, and this was broken down most formally into the itemised account—Lodging and attendance: 9d. Breakfast of 6 ounces of bread, 1 pint tea, 4 ounces bacon: 7½d. Dinner of one pound meat, 8 ounces bread, 8 ounces potatoes, one pint beer: 1s 7½d. Supper of 6 ounces bread, one pint of tea, 2 ounces cheese: 4½d.

Many an amateur economist (with a few professionals and, curiously, many housewives) protested in several newspapers that this was farcical, that the War Office was paying at least 70 per cent too much. The W. O., only too glad at this uncertain moment to make almost any concessions, readily capitulated, and reduced the Soldier's Billeting Fee to 2s 3d. On no recorded occasion did the billeted soldier voice the least complaint on that account; he had after all plenty of others.

Recruiting was now running at the rate of about 20,000 a day. By the middle of November 750,000 men had enlisted in the Kitchener Armies. With the standing Army and the Colonial forces, the total strength was now almost at a million.

There was, however, great distress at the management

of the distribution of pay. In theory the shilling-a-day principle had promised most private soldiers, after deductions, 6s 8½d a week clear; for this many craftsmen had readily left jobs worth up to £4 a week, which was a handsome wage. Now it was found that multitudes of men were actually being paid, after deductions, only 11d a week. Worse, there was great hardship among the families and dependents, whose needs had been left behind in the confusion of the paymaster's administration and who for weeks at a time were unable to collect anything at all.

The regulation allowance for the families of private soldiers was 12s 6d for a wife, 15s for a wife and one child, up to £1 2s for a family of five, with a special London allowance of an extra 3s 6d. There were bitter public protests at the delays in payments from Arthur Henderson, Chairman of the Labour Party, from Bonar Law and Austen Chamberlain. In Parliament the Government defended itself rather weakly; many soldiers, it was said, denied paternity of children to avoid deductions.

The pensions rate was also criticised—5s for a widow, and 1s 6d a week for each child; Arthur Henderson derided this as an absurd sum, and shortly the widow's rate was raised to 7s 6d, and 12s 6d for a widow with a child. At the same time Lord Kitchener issued an instruction that caused furious offence almost everywhere: he ordered the police to supervise the attendance at public houses of all soldiers' female dependents; they were to check and oversee their behaviour, and for any report of "misconduct" or "drinking" the allowances would be withheld.

That winter the system of payments became so disorganised that the "Prince of Wales Fund" came into being as a piece of machinery to enable the income-tax-paying classes to display their combined patriotism and compassion. The combined income of that section of the community was then around £1,000,000,000 a year. In a month the total sum contributed was not quite £2,000,000.

In November England was briefly obsessed with the sudden fear of invasion. Lord Kitchener himself had urged that such a thing be prepared against at once. There was no reason to distrust his judgment; it was well known that the Germans now had at least 250,000 troops disposable for such an adventure. Winston Churchill was persuaded to station the 3rd Battle Squadron in the Forth and bring the Second Fleet to the Thames, to dispose a considerable system of blockships and mines. The population became readily infected with a sense of crisis, and public-spirited citizens formed themselves into special Emergency Committees in all the coastal towns. The atmosphere had not been known since Napoleonic times; there was something about it simultaneously dreadful and exciting.

Some serious controversy arose—apprehensive and pedantic at the same time—as what precisely were a civilian's rights and duties in the case of invasion. Lawyers pointed out that common law and the laws of war rarely correspond, and the Hague Conventions were by no means part of the municipal law of England. A handful of neighbours who armed themselves and banded together to ward off attack might well, if they survived, find themselves liable to prosecution. There was much curious professional casuistry on this point. Under Common Law, when an invasion took place the Crown could call upon all its subjects to assist in repelling the enemy, on the same principle as the sheriff might call out the entire *posse comitatus* to assist in keeping the peace or levying execution. To refuse to take part, in such a case, was of course punishable on indictment as a misdemeanour. To be sure, the Bill of Rights, the Mutiny Act, and the Army Act were all concerned to deny the Crown's right to maintain standing armies in time of peace; yet by the Prerogative the Crown could conceivably resort to conscription. So the lawyers argued, while the coastguards and the local bank managers with their Special Constable brassards and whistles peered anxiously into the cold mists of the Channel.

The carrying of arms was a right, training to use them was not. The citizen could carry arms but he must not drill. At the same time Common Law recognized the subject's duty to put down with armed force a riot that had assumed the proportions of a felony. Yet the Hague Regulations were decisive against the legality of "resistance by individual civilians," and the German legal attitude even more emphatic. The *Handbuch des Volkerrechts*, the most authoritative piece of German legal literature, warned that "free lances who operate on their own account [*auf eigene Hand*] are just as little to be regarded as legal combatants as the individual, native or alien, who with his own fist [*auf eigene Faust*] exercises force against the enemy." The official manual of the Prussian General Staff was specifically tough on francs-tireurs, warning that no groups of civilians would be recognized unless they could prove they were authorised by the belligerent state. Strange fantasies grew in Englishmen's minds: of their little bands of brothers at the vicarage barricades, presenting the invading German Army with official permission to be there, before gallantly laying down their lives upon the lawn.

Nothing however happened, and by and by the thrill died down; the war was not after all to demand of the civilian population this relieving catharsis; only the day by day endurance of meaningless and lowering "news from the Front," of the casualty lists from the countryside less than a hundred miles away that might be in another planet. (And yet there remained one fantastic circumstance; in the midst of it all, with northern France and Flanders slowly soaking in blood and despair, while in one fortnight the BEF lost 5,000 killed in desultory trench fighting, the South-Eastern and Chatham Railway was still advertising its routine London-to-Flushing service, leaving Victoria at 6:30 every evening. It is true that passports were required.

News from the front was stagnant; only at sea did the war produce sudden moments of exhilaration and frustration. Of these the one announced with the greatest satisfaction by Winston Churchill was the story of the *Emden*.

Many weeks earlier the German Admiralty had despatched its two raiding cruisers *Emden* and *Königsberg* out to East African waters. Since then the *Emden* in particular had been playing an almost legendary havoc with

Allied shipping, and by November she had already destroyed more than £2,000,000 worth of British tonnage alone. Her captain—Captain Carl von Müller, once a master in the Hansa Line—had achieved the sort of respect many individual German commanders won from the British; there was no record of his having fought other than fairly and daringly; he had always treated his prisoners with courtesy and consideration.

He had left Kiaochow early in the war, had been chased to Malacca, had dodged into the Bay of Bengal. There he sank five British merchantmen in a row, and topped this off by shelling Madras. He was immensely elusive and resourceful, intercepting radio messages, flying the flag of many nations, occasionally mounting a dummy funnel, replenishing his bunkers and storerooms from the captured ships.

Early in November the *Emden* landed a party on the Cocos Islands. The intention was to destroy the radio station operated by the Eastern Telegraph Company. Before this could be accomplished the staff of the company managed to flash a series of messages out. The *Emden* was caught and forced to fight by the Australian cruiser *Sydney*.

The *Sydney* lost three men killed. The *Emden*, driven ashore and burned, lost two hundred. Captain von Müller and his staff officer, Prince Franz Josef von Hohenzollern, were taken prisoner. They were accorded all honours of war, received respectfully and not deprived of their swords.

Meanwhile the *Emden*'s sister-raider had come to a less glorious end. She had been found by the cruiser *Chatham* lurking in shoal waters six miles up the Rufiji River on the Tanganyika coast of German East Africa, the tangle of swampy delta-mouths abounding with hippopotamus. *Chatham*'s greater draught prevented her reaching the *Königsberg*, whose crew were to be seen comfortably encamped among the dense palms on the bank. She sent a few shells into both the ship and the camp, sunk a small collier across the only navigable channel to the sea, and left the *Königsberg* bottled up in the Rufiji for the remainder of the war.

Except for the squadron of Admiral von Spee at large off the coast of Chile, the Indian Ocean and the Pacific could be considered cleared of German raiders.

This Mr Churchill announced to Parliament with pride; three weeks later he had to rise and announce the extraordinary loss of HMS *Bulwark* within yards of shore in a British port. *Bulwark*, one of the pre-Dreadnought battleships of 15,000 tons, was lying in Sheerness Harbour that November morning when her magazine exploded. It was 7.35 A.M. and the band was practising aft, when abruptly and for no reason ever thereafter established all the TNT in her armoury went up. The whole town rocked with the detonation; for days afterwards the river was strewn with debris and bodies. *Bulwark* herself sprang into two pieces, her funnels broke off, and in three minutes she had sunk. Of her company of nearly 800 men only twelve survived; the rest died, including her commander, Captain Guy Slater.

To counteract that Mr Churchill hailed with enthusiasm the chance to announce the biggest naval victory thus far: the revenge for Coronel and the destruction there of Admiral Cradock's cruiser squadron by von Spee's *Scharnhorst* and *Gneisenau*.

Vice-Admiral Sir Frederick Sturdee, flying his flag in the battle-cruiser *Invincible*, had gone to the southernmost tip of the South American continent. That first week in November he sailed to the Falklands, and with *Invincible*'s sister-cruiser *Inflexible* was waiting in the landlocked harbour of Port Stanley.

Admiral von Spee was wholly unaware that any enemy ships of that size were in the area, and when he met a squadron of British light cruisers he pursued them, not suspecting the trap. They lured him to the Falklands, and within sight of *Invincible* and *Inflexible*. The German ships turned and ran, but the British battle-cruisers held them for speed, and both outranged and outgunned them. The Germans made a gallant reply, but the *Scharnhorst* sank at one o'clock, the *Gneisenau* two hours later. At six HMS *Kent*, avenging her sister *Monmouth* at Coronel, sent the *Nürnberg* to the bottom. Some miles away from the main battle the *Glasgow* met the *Leipzig*, and set her on fire in several places. The *Leipzig* ran up a white flag at last. *Glasgow* sent out her boats to take off the survivors; either by design or the worst kind of accident the sinking cruiser fired on the rescuing party, at which the *Glasgow* sent a broadside into the *Leipzig* and blew her up.

Only the *Dresden* escaped. The British squadron lost eight men killed, fourteen wounded.

Shortly thereafter there was an official reception at

Montevideo for Admiral Sturdee, at which he made a speech. He said: "The Germans fought well. They are an excellent people, except when they are violating neutral countries and attacking undefended towns. War is a sad thing. It is a good job that they are at the bottom of the ocean."

It was Churchill's month; now he could tell the story of the British submarine B11, commanded by Lieutenant Commander Norman Holbrook, which had produced a performance quite unprecedented in that kind of sinister seafaring: she had entered the Dardanelles, dived under five successive rows of mines, and torpedoed the Turkish battleship *Messudieh*. It had been a curious kind of veteran feud —the *Messudieh* was a very old ship; nevertheless she was one-third of Turkey's total fleet; the B-class submarines were Britain's oldest variety, built by Vickers in 1905; nevertheless the B11 had eluded the Turkish torpedo boats by remaining submerged for nine hours, and returned safely —Commander Holbrook to his Victoria Cross.

Just then an incident happened that, while no more than one incidental death among tens of thousands, broke one special link with the British Army's past: Lord Roberts, the old marshal who united the BEF with the ancient military adventures of Victoria's time, died on duty. He was paying a visit to the Indian troops, of whom he was Colonel-in-Chief; he got a chill in the dank and bitter circumstances of northern France, and in two days he was dead of pleurisy. He was in his eighty-third year; he had seen his first service in the Indian Mutiny, in 1857. He was given a State funeral in St Paul's, attended by the King and every political leader. Reporting it, the German *Lokalanzeiger* printed an editorial saying: "There are in war moments in which we salute the enemy with the sabre instead of destroying him. This moment has come with the death of Lord Roberts."

This brief gleam of chivalry flickered and went out; it was not repeated, nor was much reflection of it discernible in the tense and tormented England of that time. The invasion scare had brought with it another sudden repetition of the spy-neurosis; once again enemy agents were perceived behind every hedgerow, though rarely if ever made tangible enough to charge. In Parliament, nervous and challenging questions were thrown out; more waiters were sacked; more mysterious strangers shadowed and, frequently, arrested and questioned. In Parliament the Home Secretary, Mr McKenna, said that between Aberdeen and Devonport there were, at that time, a not insignificant number of enemy aliens in residence: indeed some 771 males and 2,190 females. Great interest had been shown in the Channel Island of Herm, which was, at the time, leased to Germans. The island had been inspected, no military installations could be detected; now it was occupied by British troops, not without grave embarrassment to the fighting-line. Sir Henry Dalziel, an MP, cited the case of a naturalised Englishman who had recently visited Holland, on his passport alone, and had actually visited the German lines before returning to London. . . .

The day came in November with a sudden and alarming mutiny in the civilian internment camp at Douglas, in the Isle of Man. Mr McKenna had to inform the House that in Douglas camp some 4,000 internees had gone into riot over the quality of the food; that in the ensuing disturbance five men had been shot. A new order provided that the internees thereafter should not sit down to dinner more than a thousand at a time. . . .

To all these strange aspects of nationalism, racialism, particularism, whatever they may have been, there was a swift reaction in some sections of the press. The *Morning Post* suddenly let loose a powerful campaign of criticism and abuse against the person of Lord Haldane—Lord Chancellor of the time, temporarily in charge of the Foreign Office. The *Post*—followed shortly by others of a like persuasion—assailed Lord Haldane as a symbol first of simple fence-sitting, then of hypocrisy and even worse. Haldane was notoriously a friend of Germany, they said; he had always insisted upon that—in the days when that meant no more than the expression of a formula of normal pre-war values mutually shared that may have been tolerable, though never desirable. Now the argument was dragged up from the cuttings-library that Haldane was the man who had once been indiscreet enough to say publicly that Germany was his spiritual home. It was easy enough thereafter to say that it was Haldane who had most recklessly reduced the British resources of infantry and artillery, who had personally palmed off on the British public this inadequate notion of a Territorial Army. It was clear in the circumstances of the time that by and by Lord Haldane, like Prince Louis, would have to go, as indeed the following year he did.

Then abruptly, sooner than anyone had expected, the war struck at the soil of England herself, in what seemed even then a singularly inappropriate place.

At the beginning of September a curious mischance befell the German Navy: the light cruiser *Magdeburg* was wrecked in the Baltic, and soon after this the drowned body of a German junior officer was picked up by the Russians on their coast. On his body—in the wildly coincidental manner to which historic moments occasionally insist on clinging—were the cipher-lists and signal books of the German Navy, and the squadron maps of the German resources in the Heligoland Bight and the North Sea.

That same week the Russian Naval Attaché in London obtained an appointment with Mr Winston Churchill at the British Admiralty. He detailed the signal he had received from Petrograd: the Russians had decoded the greater part of the German messages taken from the drowned man; the Czar's Government considered that Britain, as the significant Naval power of the time, should be quickly made *au courant* with what was learned.

Britain sent therefore a ship to Russia as soon as was practicable. By the middle of October the Admiralty was in possession of the German documents, but still, as seemed inevitable in all such Service transactions, it was several weeks later, indeed well into November, before Britain got an adequate translation. By that time, of course, it was operationally too late; the Germans knew of the Allied discovery and took efficient measures to negate it. The official German histories of a later time make it quite clear that the Germans were well aware that a compromising document had been retrieved with the dead German from the *Magdeburg*, and that by no means were they prepared to overlook the fact. Naturally they changed their plans, whatever they might have been. Yet the discovery had stimulated the British to the unprecedented idea that now, for the first time since Napoleon, somebody might attack *them*.

The North Sea fell silent until the afternoon of Monday, 14th December, when Naval intelligence was alerted that the German 1st Cruiser Squadron had been sighted leaving the shelter of the Jade River behind Heligoland, with four battle-cruisers, five light cruisers, and three flotillas of destroyers. Churchill ordered coastal forces to stand by. Nothing was heard for twenty-four hours.

The morning of 16th December broke reluctantly through a thick pervasive mist that was very nearly a fog; such sun as there was fought weakly and was lost behind the dank grey haze and smirr from the east. On the cliffs beyond Scarborough the Chief Coast-guard Officer, whose name was Arthur Dean, glanced seaward at exactly five minutes past eight; to his astonishment he saw two cruisers loom in through the vapour from behind the Castle Hill towards South Bay. When they were at 600 yards range from the Castle itself they opened fire with all guns on the starboard side. They made a passage at half-speed across South Bay, deliberately and without interference of any kind, firing as they went; then they turned on their wakes and returned, firing now from the port side.

Scarborough, with its remote and detached population of elderly ladies, retired gentlemen, hoteliers, boarding-house keepers, and the tradesmen and commerce to serve them, was breakfasting, opening its shutters, reading its post, going to school, when it was abruptly hurled headlong into the war by death screaming in from the sea. The coast-guard had no time to sound any warning when the first shells whipped into the town and tore it down in sections with horrifying and unbecoming noise—disintegrating half of the Grand Hotel on the cliff-head, carrying away the gable end of the town hall, crashing into shop-fronts and bed-rooms, bringing blood and destruction to hundreds of those both too young to comprehend what could conceivably be the reason, or too old to care. The boarding-houses on St Nicholas cliff collapsed, a whole row of cottages in Stalby Road became brick and rubble in a moment. Mr John Hall, J.P., was dressing for the day when a shell howled through his walls and blew him, and his bedroom with him, into limbo. Out to sea, but only just out to sea, the cruisers coughed their missiles into the awakening town, and the mists swirling around them grew thicker with gunsmoke.

At almost exactly the same hour two cruisers appeared off Whitby, twenty miles to the north. Their first shell smashed into a field behind the Abbey, on the East Cliff. It had probably been aimed at the railway station, which lay at a bend of the harbour east of the town. Another demolished the west bay of the Abbey. A great smoking gap appeared in the houses of Esk Terrace. People swarmed into the streets, at once aghast and inquisitive; even while the whine and thud of the shells continued, the children were busy collecting warm and abrasive fragments of shrapnel.

The same thing happened at Hartlepool, yet another twenty miles up the North Sea coast. There the Germans had the uncommon fluke to hit the gasworks, which with one explosion deprived the town of all artificial light (all that day they lined up for the telegram-counter in the post office, temporarily fitted with oil-lamps, to cable relations of their safety). Furthermore the Germans sent a casual shell clean through the local branch of Lloyd's Bank.

The German cruisers kept this up for exactly half an hour, then quietly turned eastwards and homewards into the deepening grey mist, unchallenged. As they left they strewed mines behind them. (When, shortly afterwards, these mines were located by the Royal Navy they were not removed, but plotted and actually reinforced as a screen, leaving a fifteen-mile gap between Whitby and Scarborough.)

Behind them, the three towns were left picking up their dead and wounded and staring numbly at the torn masonry, at the buildings opened up like dolls' houses, at the shattered streets. Nothing like this had ever been known before in England. The bombardment of civil towns was a conception absolutely new, not to be grasped or understood in a long half hour of bewilderment and shock.

In those thirty minutes nearly 500 people of the three towns had been quickly killed.

By now, too late, the hunt was up. The Third Battle

Squadron was rushed from the Forth to prevent the Germans' escape northward; cruisers and destroyers of the Harwich Striking Force set out to join the Second Battle Squadron. Commodore Keyes was ordered to take his submarines from their stations of Terschelling into the Heligoland Bight to intercept the enemy on their way back. Between the Germans and Germany were four British battle-cruisers and six of the most powerful battleships in the world.

Then the weather, already deteriorating fast, closed in; visibility dropped from 7,000 yards at sea to 5,000, to 4,000. The British Fleet groped desperately around in the mist; by and by the visibility diminished to 1,000 yards. The German raiding vessels slipped scatheless home.

Later that day the Admiralty issued a public statement:

> At 8 A.M. three enemy ships were sighted off Hartlepool, and at 8.15 began their bombardment. They appeared to be two battle cruisers and one unidentified cruiser. The land batteries replied and are reported to have hit and damaged one of the enemy. At 8.50 all firing ceased, and the convoy sailed away. One shell fell in the Royal Fusiliers' lines and several in the lines of the 18th (Service) Battalion of the Durham Light Infantry. Casualties among troops amounted to seven killed and fourteen wounded. Some damage was done to the towns.
>
> During the bombardment, especially in West Hartlepool, people crowded the streets, and approximately twenty two were killed and fifty wounded.
>
> At the same time a battle cruiser and an armoured cruiser appeared off Scarborough and fired about fifty shots, causing damage. Thirteen casualties are reported. At

Whitby two battle cruisers fired, damaging buildings, killing two and wounding two.

Later that same evening a supplementary communiqué was sent out:

A German cruiser force made a demonstration off the Yorkshire coast. A number of their fastest ships were employed remaining for about an hour. The Admiralty take this opportunity of pointing out that demonstrations of this character against unfortified towns, though difficult to accomplish provided that a certain risk is accepted, are devoid of all military significance. They may cause some loss of life among the civilian population and some damage to private property—which is much to be regretted—but they must not in any circumstances be allowed to modify the general Naval policy which is being pursued.

The manifest untruths of the official communiqué, the bleak unpitying coldness of its tone, sent a swift wave of exasperation and indignation through the three towns. The Admiralty could treat the affair as a "demonstration," consoling itself that it was "devoid of military significance," it could "regret" the loss of life—and underestimate it by twelve times the reality—and it could in its remote way refuse to allow Scarborough to "modify its policy"; but what had it been up to that this event should have happened at all? Had the public not been led to believe that the German Fleet was safely bottled up in Heligoland; had it not been fed for months with definitions of the Royal Navy as the most powerful afloat? At the Scarborough inquest, held by Mr George Taylor, the Coroner, the phrase was said that was quickly repeated all over England, especially in coastal towns both angry and afraid: Where was the Fleet?

It was left to Mr Churchill to attempt to redeem the maladroit officialese of his department. He could not defend the operational procedure of the Navy because of Security, but he did write publicly to the Mayor of Scarborough, saying:

> We share your disappointment that the miscreants escaped unpunished. But viewed in its larger aspect, the incident is one of the most instructive and encouraging that has happened in the war. Nothing proves more plainly the effectiveness of British naval pressure than the frenzy of hatred aroused against us. It has already passed the frontier of reason. . . . Practically the whole fast cruiser force of the German Navy, including some great ships utterly irreplaceable, has been risked for the passing pleasure of killing as many English people as possible irrespective of sex, age, or condition. Whatever feats of arms the German Navy may hereafter perform, the stigma of the baby-killers of Scarborough will brand its officers and men while sailors sail the seas.

It was resounding enough stuff, but it was specious and glib and it did not satisfy. The *Times* wrote: "The Royal Navy always says it wishes the Germans would come out and fight. They have come out, and fired at our towns with impunity. What, then, does the Navy want?"

In Germany, the *Kölnische Zeitung* rubbed the dissatisfaction in:

> The attack will bring home to the English the fact that their great Fleet is unable to protect them. Their insular

seclusion has certainly the effect of rendering it difficult to make their country a theatre of war, although even in this events must be awaited. The drawback of their insular position is the vulnerability of their coasts.

The Scarborough raid made Britain momentarily more ill at ease than anything since the great retreat of the early days. Arguments appeared in the press that "in considering terms of peace when it comes a demand should be made for the trial of those who committed criminal acts during hostilities. . . . A distinction must be made between war and murder."

But that was searching too far ahead. The war stretched into the future dismally, indefinitely; in the trenches the men were putting up with worse than a single half hour of fear and sudden death. Gradually Scarborough was forgotten.

13

Fretful and uneasy, urgent, disputatious and challenging, passionately aware of its own unorthodox destiny, the world of the arts and the creative mind had, even before the war, somehow anticipated war's disintegration of values, its canonisation of violence. Those first fourteen years of the twentieth century had rung with defiance of this kind or that—in painting, in writing, in music, in all the simultaneous groupings of creation and criticism the germs of revolt spread in little cultures in Provence, in Paris, in Fitzroy Square and Chelsea and Campden Town. At the beginning of 1914 the sound and fury of the experimenters gave the artistic world the appearance of one large Left Bank, dedicated in a score of contending ways to the business of Futurism.

The new dogma had many shrines, from the avant-garde art-shop of Ambroise Vollard in the rue Laffitte to the *Salon des Independants* and the *Théâtre de l'Oeuvre*—for Paris was to the new faith what Rome was to the old—and many acolyte *Fauves* succeeding to the priesthood of Cézanne and Gauguin and Van Gogh. In London Roger

242

Fry organised them in the Grafton Galleries: from Germany came the childlike innocent nightmares of Paul Klee, from Spain the fantasies of Juan Gris and Pablo Ruiz y Picasso. Into Paris from Allegheny, Pennsylvania, came Gertrude Stein, giving her benison and patronage to the prodigies and apprentice geniuses—those who would abolish the adjective, eliminate the line, abandon form, give words their proper heretical abstractions. It was even easier in music. That April the Futurist composer Luigi Russolo brought about riots in the Teatro del Verme in Milan with his *Four Networks of Noise*. For the rest there was the new medium, the kinematograph, or Bioscope, and its accepted prophet Charlie Chaplin—and the moving picture, too, could be hailed as proper to the trends of the day, for what was more Futurist than those eccentric adventurers, those dotty policemen, the people who fell upwards and ran backwards and talked with eloquent silent mouths only to the sound of a rambling piano in the darkness?

To the arts the war itself intruded as a greater expression of human eccentricity, in form more drastic than the painters' Vorticism, or the brutal images of the New Poets, more turbulent than the *Sacre du Printemps* and more cruel than them all at once.

To the artists the war meant many things, different and simultaneous. When it came, T. S. Eliot was reading Greek philosophy at Oxford; that year he published his "preludes." The other international American, Ezra Pound, was writing Imagist verse. James Joyce, having seen *Dubliners* emerge at last, went off to wrestle with *Ulysses* in

Zurich. And that August the twenty-nine-year-old son of a Nottingham miner, David Herbert Lawrence, was travelling with his German wife Frieda from Westmoreland to, of all places, Barrow-on-Furness. He saw the trains filled with soldiers and the workers filing into Vickers; he said: "This is simply hell." He was to find trouble wherever he went with the spy-hunters and their hostility to Frieda. For a while he took refuge in the ivory tower of the intelligentsia, Garsington, in Oxfordshire, the county home of Lady Ottoline Morrell, as did Aldous Huxley and Lytton Strachey and Katherine Mansfield and James Stephens and Walter Sickert and Virginia Woolf and Mark Gertler —all for a while.

To doubt the values of the war was to adopt the accepted intellectual view; how so abruptly could one readjust the sense of right and wrong? To Lawrence the war was the humiliation of the individual, as to Rupert Brooke it was his romantic apotheosis. To Bertrand Russell it was the corruption of the mind. To Henry James, already in his seventies, it was "a stupid disfigurement of life and an outrage to beauty." Others were more perverse—like Gaudier-Brzesca, who had escaped from a French prison to avoid military service twelve years earlier and fled to England, and who now hastened back to volunteer, and who was dead within the year, killed in the attack on Neuville St Vaast.

If you were *Fauve*, you could scarcely complain. The landscape the war was rapidly to create throughout north France and Flanders was, at least, undeniably Cubist. Nash and Nevinson painted it—accurately, grimly, starkly, Futuristically; in the ugliness of its shapes and the bitter harshness of its colouring they found the simple soldiers had produced what the Left Bank boys had sought so hard: the cult of "Dynamism."

Many entered the war themselves eagerly, reluctantly, with either curiosity or panache; there was romance of a kind, it seemed. Guillaume Apollinaire joined the artillery as a driver-gunner—philosophically, expressing it with sceptical resignation: "All the same—it is not the artists' affair to fight, or intelligence will go with everything else. They made war all through the 17th century, but Corneille and Racine did not fight, nor did Pascal or Bossuet. We do our duty as well as the rest, but really it ought to be otherwise."

Just nine years before, the Jewish scientist Albert Einstein had propounded a mathematical principle, incomprehensible to most people, on the Theory of Relativity. Shortly before that a Jewish doctor, Sigmund Freud, had set forth in *Die Traumdeutung* his theory of the interpretation of dreams, an argument almost as baffling in its novelty. Two years later Louis Blériot had climbed into a flying-machine at Sangatte in Picardy and astonished the world by flying across the Channel. Graham White, another mad aviator, staggered through the air from London to Manchester to win Lord Northcliffe's prize of £10,000, offered by the *Daily Mail* to the first man to accomplish this bizarre feat. The mind, the soul and the body had never enjoyed such accelerated attention. Now Europe dragged itself numbly through December towards the first Christmas of World War, and soul and body inhabited different spheres. The Vatican issued an appeal from the Pope urging that a truce be held over Christmastime; the proposal was ignored officially, though indeed the notion was to develop spontaneously in the heart of the war itself.

Halfway through December, after a long period of uneasy pause, the fighting in France broke out again—not hugely, or dramatically, but in bitterly desperate local encounters all along the line. British airmen threw some bombs on the German installations at Bruges, and again at Freiburg in Baden. On the 17th, Joffre gave the order to advance along the line between Ypres and the River Lys. Some little mounds were taken, a few fields changed hands: "Progress was made." Trench warfare was now a struggle for *yards* of ground, and the landscape between the lines ceased to bear any resemblance to that of any inhabited country—not a tree now stood intact for many scores of miles; their bleak stumps rose spectrally from a gelid swamp. The rain was incessant, and the flooded Yser spread among the trenches indiscriminately in rivers of mud, though the Germans were worse off since their positions were on lower ground. What with the rain and the inundations the whole plain of Saint-Georges was under water. The Germans had been established many weeks there, and at Lombaertzyde near Nieuport; the trenches between Nieuport and Nieuport-Bains were separated from the French and Belgians only by the twenty yards of the canal.

The Belgians suddenly appeared in a novel motorised three-man machine-gun they called "*la Mouche-guêpe*"— the "wasp-fly"—skating and slithering around in the mud and ice. The observer sat on the conning tower, the gunner and driver were enclosed, and the *équipe* was as hard to hit as a rocketing pheasant.

(It was largely believed in England at the time that the BEF was sustaining the whole, or at least the major part of the German pressure, while the French either looked on or moved off. In fact during the first nine months of the war the British held a front of 30 miles on average, and the French held almost 500 miles.)

For days an artillery barrage along the line of the Vosges was violent enough to be heard in Switzerland. In Lorraine the war ebbed and flowed forever over the same ground, which began to seem in appearance barely terrestrial; for a long time neither side could venture to collect its dead and wounded. Men lay bleeding for days, gangrenous and verminous; in one sector thirst became so terrible that men drank their own urine, and French and Germans raved and mumbled together in delirium.

The co-operation between the French and the BEF improved, became formalised to a pattern of tolerance at the worst, comradeship at the best. Such stubborn villagers as remained among their ruins, watching their houses being commandeered for billets or demolished to make a field of fire, shrugged and said, "*Nous préférons que vous soyez ici que les Allemands.*"

Some spirited anecdotes and legends grew—of the

Gurkhas who performed feats of unspeakable dexterity and horror with their *kukris;* of a Canadian platoon who took 100 yards of trench armed only with entrenching tools; of the British aviator who, forced down behind the enemy lines, held up a German repairs-unit and compelled them to mend his engine.

One authenticated *jeu d'esprit* came from a French sector where, it seemed, an extremely important message had to be carried to the battery commandant through heavy fire and torrential rain. The infantry captain, unable to find a motor-cycle despatch-rider, was reluctant to send a foot-runner through such terrible conditions. A private came forward, however, and volunteered to carry the despatch, suggesting that he might in the circumstances be the speed-iest means of delivering it—as indeed he had reason to feel, since he was Henri Siret, the French Olympic runner and holder of several long-distance records. He cut across the streaming fields, covering the ground with a curious loping stride. No bullet hit him, and he finished the distance of al-most eight miles in just over forty-five minutes.

Life began to return to Paris, as also did the Govern-ment. Just as the retreat of the administration to Bordeaux had marked the nadir of French fortunes, so did the return of the Government to Paris allow the city to re-establish its morale as the capital of France. The music-halls and *cafés-chantants* opened again, and there was perhaps more than usual singing of patriotic songs, with a desparate sincerity, to exorcise the sense of guilt that one could sing at all when men were dying *la-bas*, as the long casualty lists made every Parisian only too bitterly aware.

There flew in from the east the occasional Taube, throwing the occasional bomb. Every week the Germans threatened that the new Zeppelin squadrons were ready to attack Paris, and the police, taking this possibility very seriously, practiced their bugle-call air-raid alarms with such zeal and persistence that the population came to accept the warning rehearsal as one more permanent addition to the stridency of Paris life.

At last the British soldiers were arriving in Paris for the first time; the Parisians were entranced by the sight of the kilt: even more beguiling than the cloak of the Spahis or the cavalry cuirasses. The city became peopled with novel and curious personalities—Zouaves, Highlanders, Hindus with spectacles and Muslims with orange hajji beards, wealthy dutiful women driving ambulances, tall Anglo-Saxon nurses in breeches on their way to the hospitals on the Riviera.

On the 22nd the Chamber of Deputies met for the first time since the war began. M. Viviani, the Prime Minister, told Parliament to tremendous applause: "France will lay down her arms only when she has avenged her outraged rights, reunited her ravaged provinces, restored heroic Belgium to the plenitude of her material life and political independence, and crushed Prussian militarism, in order to restore and reconstruct on a basis of justice a Europe at last regenerated." It was fine stirring stuff, and an almost exact transliteration of the speech Mr Asquith had made at the Guildhall the previous month.

It became known that a strong movement was afoot in Government circles to invite the Japanese Army to send an expeditionary force to France. Clemenceau supported this warmly, though others protested that it would appear a shameful sign of weakness and an impossible humiliation to French pride. Clemenceau, however, said: "It will be difficult ever to claim that our inevitable victory will be 'especially French' when it will have required the total efforts of England, Russia, Serbia, Belgium, and the coming intervention of Italy, Rumania, and Greece."

France did not get the Japanese Expeditionary Force, nor did Germany get the support of the Scandinavian state for which she had been manoeuvring. For some weeks past there had been most circumstantial reports of German feelers for some means whereby the Scandinavian countries could unite in a sort of Federation under the sovereignty of King Gustav of Sweden and the patronage of the German Empire. Now, however, the three sovereigns unexpectedly announced a meeting at Malmö—Gustav, Haakon of Norway, and Christian of Denmark. They specifically rejected this proposition, and announced instead a Triple Alliance and a treaty of mutual support in independent neutrality.

This was held in Allied circles to be a valuable pointer to the new feelings outside the combatant ring. So too was the *New York Times* editorial on December 15th which said:

Germany is now doomed to certain defeat. Bankrupt in statesmanship, overmatched in arms under the moral condemnation of the civilized world, befriended only by Austria and the Turks—backward-looking, dying nations —desperately battling with the host of three great Powers, she pours out the blood of her heroic subjects and wastes her diminishing substance in a hopeless struggle that postpones but cannot alter the final decree.

Two days after that the British made the first diplomatic move of international importance since the acquisition of Cyprus: a Protectorate was declared over the entire territory of Egypt.

This at least rationalised a situation that had been becoming more and more anomalous; not only was the Sultan of Turkey at war with the Allies, now the Khedive of Eygpt appeared to support this with whole heart. Only by an elaborate system of artifice and shifting attitudes was any sort of control over Egypt painfully administered by Britain. Most people foresaw trouble ahead with the capitulations, which was a clumsy politico-legal makeshift anyway. Now Abbas Hilmi Pasha, the Khedive, who had technically adhered to the King's enemies, was deposed from the caliphate and Prince Hussein Kemel appointed in his place, with the recorded title of Sultan. He was a prince of the family of Mohammed Ali, and was said to be tolerant, enlightened and educated. The device was shrewd and not wholly unpopular; the sultanate was to last for seven years until Hussein was succeeded by his brother Fuad, who was called King. Egypt, every British legislator knew, was at last rational, durable and loyal.

14

London watched Christmas approach with apprehensive pangs hardly relieved by the furious commercial efforts to maintain "business as usual." The first shock of wartime horror was gone but the ache not yet dulled; on another hand the first surge of exultation had slowed and foundered on the field of Mons and the Aisne. By and by the war was to be become institutional, with all life geared to its seeming endlessness, as though it were no longer an incident but life itself, but as that first Christmas approached that time had not yet come.

Yet the two worlds remained separate, incompatible, meeting only on remote terms through the newspapers, through the snatches of censored letters, at times of leave. . . . There was still no distribution of hardship; one of the worlds was "Somewhere in France," which was nightmare; the other was "Blighty," which was serene, even luxurious in its most commonplace aspects, to be dreamed of in hungry fantasies through the freezing dugout nights, to be envied almost with anger. "Somewhere in France" there were the gallants, the dedicated, the romantics, facing the wretchedness of fighting with the serene certainty of a Rupert Brooke; for the rest it was a war of the System against the individual, or even a conspiracy of the old against the young. Bitterly Siegfried Sassoon symbolised that in his "The General":

> "He's a cheery old card," grunted Harry to Jack
> As they slogged up to Arras with rifle and pack.
>
> *   *   *   *   *
>
> But he did for them both by his plan of attack.

In neither of the two worlds was it easy to maintain a consoling cynicism, even in the face of what Rainer Maria Rilke called "this dreary human muddle of trumped-up doom." For all around were miracles of bravery, decency, endurance, sacrifice, even imagination and magnificence. This was the refinement of the dilemma: why should a circumstance of which all sensitive men disapproved, hated and despised be necessary to provide proof of the real splendours of individual behaviour? Humanity's situation was desperate indeed if you could not separate good from evil, blood from generosity, slaughter and cruelty from devotion and gentleness. It was indeed no time to be a poet.

So the soldier returning to London, when so rarely he could, hurled himself readily into its prodigality, grateful for its easements while viewing its comfort with anger. For a moment, then, the "profiteer" with his war contracts, the Brass Hat in Whitehall with his nights out at Romano's, took on the semblance of enemies; sometimes the soldier reversed his longings and looked forward almost with relief to a return to the loyalties and simple wretched values of the trenches.

There were by now almost 200,000 Belgian refugees in the country. About 1,000,000 had fled their country since the war began. Holland had taken 500,000, and France about 100,000. There were also in England some 6,000 Jews from Russia and Poland, they were the charge of the various Jewish organisations.

The Belgians were a different matter, and their presence was at the same time a moral challenge and an economic problem. They were technically the responsibility of the Metropolitan Asylums Board, but as the war solidified and lengthened it became clear that some means must be found of integrating them into the country's economy. What could they do? The Belgians could not be given employment in fields where British were having difficulty in finding work. The Trades Unions were already uttering clear warnings that they would not countenance any trend to move the Belgians in at rates below the accepted pay scales. It was an unfortunate fact that the refugees were on the whole an urban population; few had either aptitude or wish to work in agriculture. It was suggested that they might be organised in colonies, grouped in country establishments that might be called "collectives." Meanwhile they waited bleakly in their dormitories and billets spread over England, thinking only of home.

There was, in fact, far less unemployment in Britain than had been feared would follow in the wake of the war. This was in some part due to the unusual needs of the war itself, the tremendous output suddenly demanded of clothing, foods, boots, arms, ammunition; it was also partially due to the organisation of labour pressed, rather quietly and discreetly, by the Government. There were some who talked darkly of "experiments in Socialism," though there was little they could cite as an example of this but the Government's scheme to establish in England the manufacture of aniline dyes.

Indeed a very serious effort was under way to profit commercially by the disruption of the war by capturing what had been German enclaves of trade. Mr Runciman hurriedly set up a series of exchange meetings between merchants and manufacturers, and arranged study-samples of German industrial products, so that the British manufacturers could examine the goods and discuss with the traders the possibility of reproducing them in quality and price. Special premises were taken in Cheapside, and every two weeks the British dealers laid their battle-plans to invade the German-occupied territory of toys, glass, china, cutlery, clocks, enamels, tinware, jewellery and haberdashery.

The first emphasis had been on toys, in view of the Christmas trade. The biggest top manufactories in the world were in Nürnberg, as everyone knew. Nobody, as far as was recorded, had ever made china dolls' heads in Britain. One of the early positive results of the war was that dolls' heads began to be made in Stoke. All the frames used in making women's handbags came from Germany; an organisation was set up to fill that want. The Germans had made practically all the cheap knives and scissors and razors in the world. Sheffield, pre-eminent for the finest cutlery made by man, turned a section of its industry to what the Board of Trade called "a certain market, particularly in Africa, for a cheap and showy article which is not necessarily durable."

It seemed clear that the war, in spite of Kitchener, might not last for ever.

The week of Christmas brought in a rush of freakish and capricious weather; for days all southern England was covered in thick and choking fog, which was suddenly and violently blown away by furious gales and blizzards, which stripped roofs from suburban houses, uprooted trees, and sank many small ships along the harbours of the East Coast. It subsided, and a terrible cold descended on the country, as though trying to suppress in depression the artificial celebrations building up around. That week one man in London found his spirits so low and his frustrations so unsurmountable that he brought an action for damages against his father, for having caused his existence and thereby, in essence, brought distress and dismay upon him. It was argued on a sound legal principle that if a man does another man an injury which the victim cannot prevent, and to which he did not give his consent, he must indemnify him. The action was, reasonably enough, withdrawn before suit.

Not all were so cast down. French visitors, arriving in London at that time, were surprised to see how little the visible social life of the city had apparently been affected by the war. The hotels and restaurants were prospering, the theatres were full. To be sure, there was khaki everywhere, but the fraction of British men embodied in the Army was inevitably smaller, and likely always to be smaller than the French; the British economic life was less disturbed. To a Frenchman in London, the Channel seemed like an ocean.

The shops were full; there was as yet no hint of rationing. Covent Garden sprouted Christmas trees at every corner; Norfolk turkeys were tenpence a pound. Debenham and Freebody's fur store was offering twenty-five guinea musquash coats with skunk collars at £18 7s 6d. *Peter Pan* was in its eleventh year, at the Duke of York's, with Madge Titheradge as Peter. Dean Inge was preaching in St Paul's; all was well in the City. An advertisement appeared in the daily papers: "Thanks to the iron grip of the British and French Fleets on the High Seas, Perrier water is being shipped safely via Marseilles as usual. Beware of German waters—Apollinaris, Johannis, Canbrunnen and the like. . . ."

At the Hippodrome *Hullo Tango!* was still running, and the delivering boys cycled about singing, "Sister Susie's sewing shirts for soldiers." Then London, at the edge of Christmas, was overtaken and invaded by Mark Sheridan's pantomime chorus, soon to spread all over France:

Here we are, here we are, here we are again!
There's Pat and Mac and Tommy and Jack and Joe.
When there's trouble brewing, when there's something doing
Are we downhearted? No!

The King and Queen moved out to Sandringham; the Asquiths to Walmer Castle. Shorn of news from the front, the newspapers briefly mourned the closing of the last horse tramcar service in London, from Tower Bridge Road to Rotherhithe. There was a merry ceremony at Victoria Station when Mr Seymour Hicks left with the first Concert Party to play base camps for the troops, with Ellaline Terris, Gladys Cooper, Ben Davies, and Ivy St Hellier. With them went the Christmas gift from the Maharajah Scindia of Gwalior to the King: a fleet of forty-one ambulances, four officers' cars, five motor lorries and ten motorcycles.

Into all this suddenly intruded a cold and sinister note, presaging things to come that had already begun to exercise the Naval planners in Winston Churchill's war-room. The *Berliner Lokalanzeiger* printed an official article by Rear Admiral Schlieper which said:

> The Germans have always been at a disadvantage with regard to England, as they could never overcome their sentimental feeling of justice and delicacy, even when other feelings would be more suitable. We waste too much time on humane things, while our enemies regularly do us harm whenever and wherever they can. Now England is waging a "business war" against us, hoping to crush us economically. We must therefore begin a systematic war of retaliation against British commerce. For this we possess the most effective tool—our submarines. Naturally this weapon must be employed not merely against hostile warships, but against *all* shipping under the enemy flag approaching British coasts. Towards an enemy like England—which knows no leniency where questions of reaching her aim are concerned, who with the greatest want of principle disowns the white race and fights shoulder to shoulder

with coloured people—to such an enemy we need show no leniency. In the submarine Germany has an advantage which must be used with all determination. . . .

On Christmas Eve England was raided from the air for the first time in her history.

That morning a small German biplane hummed in over the coast through the Channel mists and made a wide turn at no great height over Dover. As it did so a small bomb fell from it, and exploded in the garden of Mr T. A. Terson, just behind St James's Rectory, making a moderate crater and causing no harm whatever. The plane turned back into the mist.

The next day—Friday, Christmas Day—the Germans came again. At noon a monoplane was observed flying at a great height east-to-west over Sheerness, coming in from Eastchurch. There was a great fuss from the anti-aircraft batteries along the estuary, and three British aircraft took off to intercept. Great crowds, attracted by the uproar, gathered in the streets to watch the little machine glinting in the dark sky, until it wheeled away and vanished to the east, having dropped no bombs and apparently accomplished nothing except to stimulate a tumult of excitement in southern England and promote the "Anti-Zeppelin and Air War Insurance Scheme" offered by the *Daily News*.

It was by chance and not design that just as the Germans were reconnoitring the Thames on that Christmas Day the British Navy mounted its most ambitious aerial attack on the German base at Cuxhaven, at the mouth of the Elbe, 310 miles from the east coast of England. It was an operation wholly experimental and orthodox by contemporary standards; an action in several dimensions.

In broad daylight, a squadron of seven British seaplanes attacked the Cuxhaven installations and the shipping lying in the Schillig roads. They had an escort of light cruisers, destroyers, and submarines.

As soon as the Germans became aware of the attack they sent up two Zeppelins in a counter-attack, accompanied by four seaplanes. Simultaneously several submarines moved out against the British naval escort. There then ensued a complex and extraordinary combat that was to be described with some awe in the days to come as the "war of the future," and the "battle in the field of science," involving as it did ships of war at the same moment in the sky, on the sea, and below the sea.

The Zeppelins, which could become offensive weapons only by putting themselves in a very vulnerable position, were quickly driven off by concentrated anti-aircraft fire from the *Undaunted* and the *Arethusa,* nor could the German sea planes approach near enough to do damage. The British ships remained for three hours off the German coast; the cruisers re-embarked three of the seven seaplanes and their crews, and three other pilots were later picked up by prearrangement by the British submarines standing by, their aircraft being sunk. One pilot alone failed to return—Flight Commander Hewlett, son of Maurice Hewlett, the novelist.

This was held to demonstrate the curious possibilities of the hydroplane, until then a very speculative instrument. (It was just two years since Mr F. K. McLean had been the first aviator to fly up the Thames and alight on its surface.) "The future of the air," said a commentator that week, "is assuredly at sea."

It had been exactly one century since there had been signed, in the old Carthusian monastery in the city of Ghent, the treaty of peace between Great Britain and the United States, bringing to an end the last war between the two great English-speaking nations. Long before, a centenary celebration had been planned by committees of both countries to be held on the site; now nothing could be done except an exchange of messages.

The Germans were firmly entrenched in Ghent, and for some reason had singled out the city for an especially heavy Christmas levy. The occupation garrison ordered the city to provide for their use 1,000,000 cigars, 90,000 pounds of tobacco, and the contents of every commercial wine-cellar. They even commandeered 12,000 musical instruments. Throughout Belgium they suddenly imposed a curiously capricious tax: every poultry-keeper in the country had to pay an impost of twenty-five centimes per fowl per month.

One year before throughout the Belgian towns of Brussels, of Malines, of Liége, of old Namur and Louvain the streets had been crowded with the Christmas processions round the crowded churches and the glutted shops. Now the churches were ruins and the altars dark, the houses standing empty and cold, the people moving blankly among the silent walls.

From the German Commands went out laconic messages of Christmas cheer and encouragement. "Continue in cold blood," wired the Crown Prince. Von Kluck, even more economically, said: "Continue." Von Tirpitz told his Fleet: "Forward." The Crown Prince of Bavaria's message said: "No words and wishes, but Will and Work."

That Christmas Eve along many miles of the entrenched front there was to be observed a curious phenomenon: along the parapets of the German positions appeared rows of small lights, and across the tormented frozen mud of no-man's-land came a sound few soldiers had heard for many months—the sound of men's voices singing hymns. After a while it paused, and there was complete silence; by and by the singing began again, louder, and the lanterns were raised above the trench-tops on the points of bayonets. Very soon the numbed and doubtful soldiers of the BEF and the French saw the Germans climb one by one from their trenches, singing and signalling as they sang. They themselves then climbed out, leaving their rifles behind them, and very soon there were many hundreds of men, many thousands of men between the Channel and the Vosges, meeting together and greeting one another in what words they could contrive, exchanging gifts and sharing cigarettes. This was the Christmas truce that the Commands had refused; it was the subject of many disciplinary measures and it was never to happen again.

Great battles were continuing far to the East, as the German Army leaned its weight on Warsaw, shelling the huge tenements of Sochaczew and Lowicz; down in Galicia

their front moved steadily forward along the River Duna-
jec; slowly the Russian steamroller gave way, bogged down
in its own blood.

So 1914 came to an end, with the customary communiqué from French Headquarters: *"A l'ouest, rien à
signaler"*—"All quiet on the Western Front."

Down the long arc of wretchedness from Picardy to
the mountains the men waited among the mud and the ice,
the gun-limbers and the vermin. Very soon the horizons
would open up again; someone in Whitehall or the Invalides
would press the button again and they would climb—wearily, angrily, fearfully, gloriously—over the parapet again,
and what would happen then no one could say.

BIBLIOGRAPHY

Especially valuable among the many books consulted were:

"Twenty-five Years," by Lord Grey (Hodder & Stoughton); "The Private Papers of Douglas Haig" (Eyre & Spottiswoode); "World Crisis 1914–1918," by Winston Churchill (Macmillan); "Liaison 1914" by Sir Edward Spears (Heinemann); "Life of Lord Oxford and Asquith," by J. A. Spender and Cyril Asquith (Hutchinson); "A North Sea Diary" by Stephen King-Hall (Newnes); "The Soul of the War," by Philip Gibbs (Heinemann); "At the End of the Day," by Viscount Maugham (Heinemann); "Haig," by Duff Cooper (Faber & Faber); "The Unfolding Pattern of British Life," by E. Wingfield-Startford (Hale); "King George V," by Harold Nicolson (Constable); "Memories and Reflections," by Lord Asquith (Cassells); "The Strange Death of Liberal England," by George Dangerfield (Constable); "Manifest Destiny," by Brian Connell (Cassell); "Panorama 1900–1914," by Harold Herd (Allen & Unwin); "A Portrait of Britain," by Donald Lindsay and E. S. Washington (Oxford); "Oxford History of England 1870–1914," by R. C. K. Ensor (Oxford); "The March of the Moderns," by William Gaunt (Cape); "Great Morning," by Osbert Sitwell (Macmillan); "Mutiny at the Curragh," by A. P. Ryan (Macmillan); "History of Modern Europe," by G. P. Gooch (Cassell).

... INDEX

272